Brimming with creative inspiration, how-to projects, and useful information to enrich your everyday life, Quarto Knows is a favorite destination for those pursuing their interests and passions. Visit our site and dig deeper with our books into your area of interest: Quarto Creates, Quarto Cooks, Quarto Homes, Quarto Lives, Quarto Drives, Quarto Explores, Quarto Gifts, or Quarto Kids.

© 2020 Quarto Publishing Group USA Inc.
Text © 2020 Tom Madigan

First Published in 2020 by Motorbooks, an imprint of The Quarto Group, 100 Cummings Center, Suite 265-D, Beverly, MA 01915, USA.
T (978) 282-9590 F (978) 283-2742 QuartoKnows.com

Motorbooks titles are also available at discount for retail, wholesale, promotional, and bulk purchase. For details, contact the Special Sales Manager by email at specialsales@quarto.com or by mail at The Quarto Group, Attn: Special Sales Manager, 100 Cummings Center, Suite 265-D, Beverly, MA 01915, USA.

24 23 22 21 20   1 2 3 4 5

ISBN: 978-0-7603-6599-1

Digital edition published in 2020
eISBN: 978-0-7603-6600-4

Library of Congress Cataloging-in-Publication Data

Names: Madigan, Tom, 1938- author.
Title: Mickey Thompson : the lost story of the original speed king in his own words / By Tom Madigan.
Description: Beverly, MA : Motorbooks, an imprint of The Quarto Group, 2020.
Identifiers: LCCN 2019029363 (print) | LCCN 2019029364 (ebook) | ISBN 9780760365991 (hardcover) | ISBN 9780760366004 (ebook)
Subjects: LCSH: Thompson, Mickey, 1928-1988. | Drag racers--United States--Biography.
Classification: LCC GV1032.T55 M33 2020 (print) | LCC GV1032.T55 (ebook) | DDC 796.72092 [B]--dc23
LC record available at https://lccn.loc.gov/2019029363
LC ebook record available at https://lccn.loc.gov/2019029364

Cover and interior design: James Kegley
Page Layout: James Kegley
Front and Back Cover Images: Don Gillespie
End paper photos courtesy of Greg Sharp

Printed in China

MICKEY THOMPSON

THE LOST STORY OF THE ORIGINAL SPEED KING IN HIS OWN WORDS

TOM MADIGAN | FOREWORD BY ALEX XYDIAS

motorbooks

DEDICATION

Dedicated to the memory of Mickey and Trudy Thompson.

Dedicated also to the late Gary Campbell and to Collene Campbell (Mickey's sister).

To Danny Thompson for keeping his father's tradition of record-breaking speed in the family.

CONTENTS

PREFACE

Like nearly every accomplishment made throughout his life, Mickey Thompson faced every challenge without fear and with very little compromise. This book is no exception. In his life, Thompson went his own way, pushed limits, bent many rules, and never let the words "it can't be done" get in his way. When the going got tough, Mickey's favorite comeback was always, "Adjust."

This project follows in the spirit of the Thompson legacy: it bends the rules, offers a challenge to the reader, and follows its own path, just the way Mickey would have wanted it to play out.

FOREWORD BY
ALEX XYDIAS

Author's Note: Well into his nineties, Alex Xydias carries the history of hot rodding from its earliest days. From the California dry lakes to the inception of drag racing as a sport, Alex was there. He was one of the founders of the speed equipment industry when he opened So-Cal Speed Shop shortly after World War II. Alex is a true founding father of the sport.

I guess the best place to begin is at the beginning. As a child, I can imagine Mickey Thompson looking at the chain on his bicycle. He was curious: "How did it work?" And his next thought was, "How can I make it better?"

As years passed, in addition to being curious, he became inventive, competitive, hardworking, a dreamer, a junkyard raider, a speed seeker, an engine builder, a record setter, and a true legend. Later in life, Mickey succeeded as a big event producer and promoter, an incredible showman, and a genius for knowing what the crowd wanted to see.

Number one on the list of attributes Mickey was well known for was being a competitor.

Like all of us humans, Mickey had a flip side. He was hardheaded and stubborn, and when he thought he was right there was not much you could do to stop him. Mickey had his own set of rules that he lived by, and if you didn't agree, then you had to convince him why. He also had a bit of a temper. If push came to shove, Mickey was not the one to walk away from a fight. It was this attitude that made him successful. You can't be a champion without an ego, a strong drive to win, and a will to overcome any obstacle. Mickey loved to put on a show, and his actions were sometimes over the top, but people accepted him as he was and respected his abilities and his willingness to push the limits.

Whenever I experienced Mickey's other side, I would always hold off judgment until I understood the whole story and his real motives. Most of the time he was right, and we would agree and then charge ahead.

I remember hearing a tape recording that Mickey had made for an interview when he said, "Back when I was going to school, I was in the minority. When you were Irish and your father was a cop, fighting wasn't a traumatic experience; it was a way of life." And then Mickey added, "There is one thing that I would never do and that is walk across the street to change someone's opinion of me. If they think one particular way about me, then they can believe that way forever for all I care."

That was the way Mickey felt, take it or leave it.

I remember a song a few years back about no mountain high enough that can't be climbed. That fit Mickey to a T: there was never a mountain too high for him to climb.

As an example, the Mexican 1000 Off-Road Race is run over the wilds of Baja and some of the toughest terrain you can ever find. So bad is the course that it makes Mars look like a parking lot. But for Mickey there was not enough dirt and rocks in all of Baja to stop him. He pre-ran the course over and over, making maps of the bad spots so on race day he could just run flat out, pedal to the metal.

Another example was his desire to run 400 miles per hour over the Bonneville Salt Flats with the help of a few friends, so he created the fabulous four-engine *Challenger* streamliner and became the first American to run 400 miles per hour.

He had a tremendous impact at the Indy 500. Ask any professional drag racer and they will tell you that Mickey created a long list of innovations in Top Fuel and Funny Car, as well as offering many a young driver the chance to become a superstar.

Mickey brought off-road racing out of the wilderness and into venues like the Los Angeles Coliseum and Riverside International Raceway to give the fans an up close and personal feel for the action. I worked for and with Mickey for many years and found the time to be filled with excitement and energy. Mickey and his wife Trudy are gone now, and there will always be a void in the racing world from their passing. One thing is for sure, though: Mickey Thompson will always have a place in my heart.

Enjoy this long-overdue story of Mickey and his early days on his way to becoming an auto racing icon.

SID COLLINS
REMEMBERS MICKEY THOMPSON

Author's Note: Long before the computer, iPhone, flat-screen TV, and limitless reach of social media, there was a magic box in most living rooms from which poured imagination. It was called radio. In the world of auto racing, radio played a very important role in bringing the color and action of the event to life. As a young boy in the years after World War II, I recall the days when the Indy 500 was first introduced as a nationwide radio broadcast. The action was recounted in short five-minute breaks during regular programming to offer updates on the progress of the race. It was not a perfect method, but it was all that was available.

In 1952, Sid Collins took the Indy 500 mainstream and, for the first time, the entire race, from green flag to checker, the 500 was broadcast live on what would be called the Indianapolis Motor Speedway Network. Sid and his band of announcers brought the color and action to the racing fan. Once you heard the program you were hooked. You had to listen, then convert the words into vision, and your mind would produce the roar of the engines, the flashing color of the cars, and the thrill of the battle. To this day, I can still remember the descriptions presented by Sid and his colleagues as they would call out to each announcer located around the 2 ½-mile track: Jim Shelton in the north turn, Luke Walton in the pits, Bill Frosch in the south turn, and former 500 winner Mauri Rose in the press box with Sid. (Mauri Rose would be replaced by Indy driver Freddie Agabashian in later years.)

From 1948 until the early 1970s, Sid Collins was the most famous voice in American auto racing. His annual Indy 500 radio broadcasts were heard over more

9

than 1,200 radio stations worldwide with 100 million listeners. Sid's years in front of the microphone became the largest single-day sporting event in the country.

Sid Collins is gone, but his memory is still around, tied to an announcement he made famous. Who can forget the words of Sid every time a break in the program was taken? He'd say, "Stay tuned for the greatest spectacle in racing."
Here, then, is a voice from the past and the lost memories of Sid Collins about his friend Mickey Thompson.

Here in the Midwest we love auto racing. Many of us were weaned on the small ovals at Winchester, Salem, New Bremen, and Terre Haute. As kids we all wanted to go to the Indy 500. I was one of those kids whose glorious opportunity came some years later after I had become an apprentice radio announcer and was given the chance to work on the early 500-Mile Race broadcast crew.

Since that day, my life has been wrapped up with the daring souls who run fast in any possible manner. My true pleasure has come from knowing firsthand what sort of people they are. I am fortunate to number many as my close friends, and among those is a man who was making headlines every week when we met in early 1950: the unparalleled Mickey Thompson.

I shall not belabor the details here, because these points will be recounted on the pages that await you. But the following are a few of the memories that I equate as synonymous with the name Mickey Thompson. Number one, the first slingshot dragster called the *Lakewood Muffler Special* that roared down the quarter-mile at 150 miles per hour and made up in performance what it lacked in appearance. Mickey set the one-way land speed record at the Bonneville Salt Flats. He created the first American-built rear engine car of the modern era to run at Indy. He was involved in the development of the low-profile, extra-wide racing tire and safety equipment like water-filled safe barriers for racetracks and other products. He built a drag strip so young racing enthusiasts would have a place to go without worrying about the dangers of street racing and the long arm of the law. He loved young people and had a personal crusade against drug and narcotics addiction.

The human side of Mickey was not always so easy to see by those who have run up against his occasional brusqueness. When he had a goal, he'd be gunning after he ran his own interference, and one could get caught in the undertow.

I believe that the Mickey Thompson character can be best summed up in the following little story. One year at Indianapolis, a few days before race day, I had invited Mickey to stop by our broadcasting booth during the actual race and do an interview. After the invitation was sent, I found out that he was in a stiff back brace and was in much pain due to a broken back he had suffered in a crash at Bonneville. I mentally crossed off his appearing because we were on the third level of the master control tower high above the start/finish line and there was no elevator.

On race day, I remember that we had reached the midpoint when the state police guard handed me a card stating that Mickey Thompson was outside as promised for the interview. When the door opened, he came in accompanied by a hospital nurse who had been assigned to him just in case he passed out from the heat of the day. Later I told him that the interview hadn't been imperative, that I merely wanted to offer the courtesy and have his millions of fans hear from him. Mickey, in his simplistic and honest way, stated a blunt truth of his: "I said I'd be here, didn't I?" And that to me said it all. I am just Hoosier minded enough to revere that sort of dedication to a promise no matter how irrelevant. Integrity is rapidly becoming a lost art, but happily some still have it.

Over two decades ago, when we first met, Mickey was running the Lions Drag Strip in Long Beach, California. Since then, this legend of mechanical genius has set over 480 national and international racing records, more than anyone else in the world.

This brings me full circle back to the beautiful hills of southern Indiana where I began. The checkered flag signifies that one has finished, and I have.

INTRODUCTION
THE STORY WITHIN THE STORY

I decided that my original introduction to *Mickey Thompson*, written in the early 1970s, would just not fit in today's world, so I took a different approach. It is my intention to present this long-gone piece of history with just a short story of how everything came together and then present this memory as it was when originally written.

Mickey Thompson was born to an era long gone from the high-tech world of today. He lived in the very beginnings of the sport we call hot rodding. When Mickey and I sat down with a tape recorder back in 1970, neither of us knew what the future held. Any attempt to update, alter, or add to the content of the book would prove to be a disservice to the true story. I hope the reader understands that it was a time that is now gone by and should simply be enjoyed as a segment of history and a learning experience to be cherished. Enjoy the ride.

Out from the Shadows

It goes without saying that a story that has lain dormant for more than forty years will need a little explanation for those who are going to read it. This particular story is no exception.

The process began in 1970. Although I had known Mickey Thompson since the late 1950s, most of our relationship had surrounded his managing Lions Drag Strip in Long Beach, California. By the mid-1960s I had gone from spectator to competitor, joining forces with the fuel dragster team of Paul Pfaff and Dave Sowins as a crew member. Shortly thereafter I went on my own with a Kent Fuller–built dragster and Dave Sowins as my mentor.

In late 1968 I moved from racer/car owner to becoming a working automotive magazine editor, and my relationship with Thompson changed. I began covering stories of Mickey's exploits and, on several occasions, went with him as a guest in his Ford Mustang program at the Bonneville Salt Flats, where he and Danny Ongais set twenty-four endurance records. At one point they ran a big-block Mustang and a small-block Mustang for a twenty-four-hour period to establish one of the records. During that run, in the middle of the night, Mickey invited me to go for a ride around the marked course at 150 miles per hour plus. Mickey could create great stories.

As the 1970s began, so did the popularity of a new form of racing called off-road that was run on wild backcountry trails in places like Baja, Mexico, and the deserts of Nevada and California. Thompson joined in the fun of this new adventure and I followed, moving from *Popular Hot Rodding* magazine to a new title called *Off-Road*.

Above: (Left to right) Thompson, actor and occasional racer James Garner, and Tom Madigan at the grand opening of drag racer and famed upholsterer Tony Nancy's Sport of Wheels shop.

Previous pages: Author Tom Madigan (left) with Mickey Thompson mid-1970s.

Not content with just racing off-road, Mickey took over the promotion of major events, including Baja, and at the same time we had become good friends. It was that friendship that led to a meeting between Mickey and me where he discussed his visions of the future. He had started his own off-road association called SCORE (Short Course Off-Road Events). He wanted to expand from point-to-point racing, like the Mexican 1000 and the Baja 500, to closed-course events at established racing venues like Riverside International Raceway. It would give paying spectators a chance to witness the action up close and personal.

His second planned vision was to record in a book or manuscript all of his accomplishments, including his land speed records at Bonneville, his challenges at the Indy 500, his drag racing career, the businesses that he had started, and all of the innovations he had brought to auto racing. In general, he wanted his story to be recorded. However, typical Mickey, he wanted to hold the story until later in his life, with the idea of a movie off in the distance.

In 1972, after a few more meetings and serious talk, Mickey made me an offer and I agreed, no contract, just a handshake. I would write the words and hang on to the story until he was ready. Upon completion of the project and an OK from Mickey and his wife Trudy, I placed my original copy in a plastic container and put it in safekeeping. The years went by and life turned its pages for both me and Mickey; the buried manuscript was put on a back burner while living life took center stage.

On Wednesday, March 16, 1988, I received a telephone call early in the morning from a friend who asked whether I had heard the news. Mickey Thompson and Trudy had been murdered at their home in Bradbury, California.

The Mickey Thompson story that we had done together was lost. I would never write a word about the events in 1988 that was covered in newspapers, TV, and books over the years. The lost story was of Mickey's early days and his many victories, and I wanted it to remain as it was.

In 2018, I uncovered the original version of the story and happened to mention my discovery to Motorbooks publisher Zack Miller, whom I had worked with on several projects. He was interested, and so the story was reborn. I hope that readers will understand that the style and content is early 1970s and a lot has changed since then, but it is a personal story that needs to be told about one of auto racing's icons.

Forever Fast!
Tom Madigan

THE QUEST FOR SPEED BEGINS

It took nearly an hour to locate the house. Hazy directions combined with little knowledge of the area accounted for the time lapse. I couldn't help wondering about the scene set before me; the neighborhood was modest, and the homes seemed a bit dowdy at best. A long driveway led from the street to the front door of a small but well-manicured home. A twinge of uncertainty filled my mind as I approached the door, tape recorder and notebook in hand. The breeze of uneasiness blew a little harder as I thought about the project at hand. First, I had picked a subject that had already been done to death, the life of a race car driver. Second, the life of this particular racing personality had appeared in print a few years back. So, was the world ready for an instant replay?

Buzzing the doorbell relieved some of my pent-up emotions. The door swung open and a small, gray-haired woman stood before me. Her body was bent slightly, and I noticed a few tiny brown age spots on her hands as we clasped in greeting. Although age had notched the years on her body, the woman's voice, crisp and clear, somehow imbued the feeling that beneath her senescent exterior, a mind that was filled with awareness and an alert wit functioned near the point of flawlessness.

After the usual introductions we sat at a tiny kitchen table and I proceeded to explain my purpose for rekindling an interest in the life of her only son, at one time the fastest man on wheels in the world. My reasons were simple enough. I wanted to explore the inner workings of such a man and find out what makes him function. I wanted to separate fact from fiction, truth from rumors. I felt sure that in this controversial character beats the heart of an average, believable human being. It was some type of superior driving force, maybe a force that is instilled in everyone only to surface on a rare occasion, that produced his type of flamboyant personality and the strange ability to do anything to which he set his mind, no matter how farfetched or physically impossible. I wanted to explore these deep-rooted reasons, for only then would my own quest be fulfilled.

With a certain subtleness, Mrs. Geneva Thompson assured me that with her French and Dutch ancestral background and the few years left for her in this life cycle, the truth was foremost in her mind.

Geneva sat down at the informally set dining room table. She suggested coffee and remarked that she couldn't see as well as she used to. Thick eyeglasses covered her

Previous page: Marion Lee Thompson. While still an infant, he was nicknamed "Mickey" by a family friend.

Mickey's father was a police officer in Alhambra, California. Here Mickey tries out some of the tools of that trade.

sky-blue eyes and clouds dimmed their vision, one completely. "That's the only thing I regret," she said. "These cataracts prevent me from painting." She motioned toward a buffet that housed a complete set of very exquisite hand-painted china. Ringed with wild roses, the cups and saucers were as daintily sketched as any found in the finest shops. She motioned with a rather sad roll of her head and remarked that her project had recently concluded. I knew I was in the presence of a truly talented person.

Undaunted by stage fright, Mrs. Thompson picked up the microphone fitted to my tape recorder and began to speak. Her tone was soft and reassuring, as if the role of mother was still warm in her heart.

"Mickey was born in December of 1928, my Christmas present. It was about the only thing I could expect. Those were the Depression years and things were hard for everyone. People actually stood in bread lines. And there were many families near starvation. Mickey's dad was a construction worker in the San Fernando area and work, although not too steady, brought in some money. It didn't go far, but at least

we had food on the table most of the time. My husband was a proud man; he looked for no handouts and refused to work on the WPA, a work project set up for those less fortunate than us. He struggled, but for him having a son was the one thing that made him a rich man. I remember how tall he seemed to walk after Mickey was born. Those terrible gray times seemed to brighten somehow.

"Mickey's dad's name was Marion, as Irish as the Blarney stone. He named Mickey Marion too, Marion Lee to be exact, only changes were to begin early in life for Marion Junior." With a slight parting of her lips, she continued. "A friend of my husband's, his name avoids me now, saw Marion Lee in the hospital and spying his long red hair laughed uproariously, saying, 'There's a Mick Irishman if I ever saw one.' From that day till now Mickey was Mickey.

"When Mickey and I came home from the hospital our old house became overcrowded. It was small to begin with—houses in that area of San Fernando were extremely humble—and to compound our situation we shared the three-bedroom dwelling with my husband's mother and father. Times grew even more difficult for the first eighteen months and it seemed as if we would never see good times again. Three years later, Mickey's sister Collene was born. This forced Marion's parents to find other accommodations, but we still felt cramped; it didn't really matter, though, because we loved each other and that has a tendency to make the most disintegrative state of affairs easier to bear.

"Because times were so arduous, we didn't have much money to entertain ourselves and it seemed that my husband and I directed our attention toward Mickey. We exploited him and continually made his behavior the center of attraction." As the old woman talked it seemed that she fell into a spell of regression. Age relinquished its dulling, tight-fisted grip on her and slowly the relaxed atmosphere of recalling her role as a mother rejuvenated her spirit. She continued, and as the words came forth her once-beautiful eyes seemed to clear ever so faintly. "I suppose our spoiling him as a child is one of the reasons that he is so cocky now. But he had such unusual abilities that you just couldn't help treating him like an adult. I remember that for one reason or another we checked Mickey's IQ when he was about five years old and the doctor that conducted the tests couldn't believe that a child so young could have a score so high. I can't recall the exact digit, but I think the figure was about 149 points, or however they compound those figures. Anyway, it was substantially above average.

"Mickey was a toddler, talking much faster than he walked, when we moved to Alhambra, California, and his father left his construction job and joined the police department in Alhambra. It was a much more secure job considering the times and how hard it was for a man to gain a respectable position. To us at the time the police department seemed a salvation.

"For Mickey, the first years in our new location were happy times because with his father gone an appreciable part of the day and many instances long into the night, he could spend his time outside in the backyard building and experimenting. This is one of the strangest facets of my son's life." Just for a moment a bewildered glance crossed the face of Mrs. Thompson and I think, for the first time since we met, both of us knew we were dealing with someone whose inner fervor and capacity to drive the soul would remain aloof and evasive to all who grew too near. "He never played with toys like other children; I mean with store-bought things like games and guns, soldiers and those tiny cars that boys always seemed to carry everywhere they went. He had walked and talked by the time he was ten months old and from that point on he never stopped.

"Instead of toys, as I said, he would spend hours and hours disassembling old radios. He was absolutely fascinated by their inner workings. Wires—common, old, used household wires—held a particular engrossment for Mickey. His father once had a load of beach sand dumped into the backyard and Mickey immediately took position. After days of strenuous work, he had tunneled catacombs throughout the pile of sand and inside each tunnel he had strung hundreds of feet of wire. To him the project was real, and each wire had a meaning. Sometimes I would sit and watch in wonderment at my deep-thinking child working as if trained by some spirit for accomplishments far beyond his years.

"As Mickey grew in size, so did his projects. From wires and old radios, he moved on to building his own washing machine motor–powered wooden cars." For a moment Mrs. Thompson stopped and seemed to collect some faraway image, then she began again. "This was the first time I saw Mickey's undaunting determination against overwhelming odds, this building the little electric cars." Sensing some relative importance, something that would play a part later on in the story, I let her continue. "You know there were some rich little buggers that lived in the neighborhood and they had everything their spoiled hearts wanted, including miniaturized, gasoline-powered toy cars. Well, needless to say, they didn't like the poor kid from down the street bringing in a homemade car built from orange-crate wood powered by an old washing machine motor."

The old woman came to life again; she straightened in her chair, disregarding a cup of coffee that rested near her hand, and she began to defend her son as if the story she was telling happened in the present. "You know, there was an old abandoned house, called the Alhambra Castle by the kids. Every neighborhood has one, I'm sure. Well, the kids would tow their midget cars to the top of the driveway that wound down to the street from the entrance. Then they would race just as fast as they could to the bottom. Mickey began to drag his hand-built vehicles to the Castle

Though Mickey is clearly enjoying himself here, this form of horsepower would not satisfy him for long.

and at first the other boys would laugh at Mickey's contraptions in a most contemptuous way." Quickly, as if I had forgotten, Mrs. Thompson reiterated, "He was only a small child of seven or eight and I'm sure you know that children of that age can be exceptionally cruel when they have the advantage over someone."

She continued, "Mickey looked so helpless trudging up that hill just about every day, only to come home bewildered and filled with abandonment. He even cried on occasion. But his tenacity soon began to show itself. With the salt from his tears still drying on his cheeks he set out to beat those other boys. I was engrossed just watching him, and I even went as far as to slip him a few dollars. If his father would have found out I had given Mickey money to build a midget car when there was barely enough money to make ends meet and to keep food on the table there would have been hell to pay. Guided by some inner direction, Mickey began to plan and build. He quickly learned that the washing machine motors were the cause of the problem, so they were traded for automobile starter motors and two or three junk batteries hooked in a series. He then rebuilt his wobbling, discarded wagon wheels with rubber hose. Soon the moment of truth came and with his chin in the air and an almost desperate look in his eyes, he headed for Alhambra Castle. There were no more tears."

Time, as a governing factor, disappeared as my frail hostess continued relating events that must have revolved over and over in her mind. Her voice grew a tiny bit weary and I suggested that we could extend our interview at a future date. She snapped back with an air of perpetuality in her manner that she wanted to go on. I

couldn't help but admire her as a person and wonder, with a second chance at life, what she could accomplish.

"The second most important incident in Mickey's childhood began to manifest itself when his father decided to take the family to Yellowstone National Park for a summer vacation. The trip included a stop at Bonneville, the salt flats where all of the land speed record runs had been made. The year was 1937 and Mickey was nine years old.

"For the longest time Mickey and his father stood on that vast expansive piece of no-man's-land and talked about things to come and about happenings of times gone by. They talked of Sir Malcolm Campbell and the famed *Bluebird Special* the car with which he had broken the land speed record. Mickey also talked about Frank Lockhart, one of his idols, and about his own urge to become the fastest man on wheels."

It was here that I broke into her train of thought with a few questions. "I can't believe that a child of nine has the ability to commit his life to a specific goal and then direct his energies toward that goal. Not at nine years of age."

With a finger of reprimand pointed in my direction, a woman filled with a mother's pride set the record straight. "Oh, I'm afraid you're wrong. Not only did Mickey predict that he would be the fastest man on wheels, but also that he would become a millionaire before he was forty. I believed him then and I believed him throughout all of his projects, including the *Challenger*. I never for one instant lost faith in his predictions. I guess it was a mother's intuition. Anyway, Mickey will be able to tell you more about the way he felt as a child when you begin talking to him; I'm only telling you what I experienced and my particular feelings as I saw my son growing up to become a man." Our discordancy ended abruptly and Geneva, as she now insisted I call her, continued. "After we had stopped at the Salt Flats, we continued on our way to Yellowstone. Within hours, the very object of Mickey's entire life, namely the automobile, would nearly end his life before it had reached the fullness of spring.

"It was a beautiful sunshiny day and Mickey's dad and I were sitting in the front seat of our car enjoying the first real vacation we had experienced in many years. Mickey was kneeling on the backseat cushion with one hand out the window slightly, holding a small paper windmill, the type mounted on a wooden stick. They were a very popular, inexpensive toy at that time. Anyway, we were all watching nature, with her mountains and rich green meadows flashing by the open windows. Suddenly, without warning, a car coming head-on swerved into us. It wasn't a grinding crash as you might think it would be, but rather a loud thud. Still, there was the sound

The bicycle looks unmodified, so it must have been a recent acquisition. Geneva with Mickey's younger sister Collene.

of broken glass and I was thrown about with a violent jarring motion. In an instant everything was silent. My first thought was of Mickey; I could see that my husband was without anything more serious than a few bruises, he had already kicked his way out of the car. The man who had hit us was drunk and had continued down the road stunned into a stupor by the deed he had just completed. Now that I think back it was eerie because for a split second my mind relaxed; I heard no screaming, therefore my mental processes concluded that my fears were without justification. As I reached for Mickey the shock of what I saw actually flashed before my eyes like a gunshot, streaks of yellow and blinding white erased the vision before me. In the blinking of an eye reality returned and I viewed my frail, loving son, his arm shattered by a compound fracture, blood oozing from the puffed and distorted limb. Shock filled his eyes, but he didn't cry. It was all I could do to keep from breaking down myself, he looked so pitiful, his arm was so torn.

Mickey and Collene with pet rabbits circa late 1930s.

"I pulled myself together, I guess it was my years of training as a registered nurse that triggered my reflex action. Grabbing Mickey, I laid him down on the soft grass next to the road and covered him with the thin cotton sweater that I was wearing. My poor child just lay there; he didn't cry, he just kept repeating over and over, 'Don't worry, Mom, let's pray.' He was the bravest child I had ever seen, not because he was mine, but because he was really trying to be a man. Mickey's father, in a fit of rage, had given chase to the man who had caused the accident. When he was angry, Mickey's dad was a most fearsome individual. He was a large, hulking man to start with and once that Irish temper was fired, he could punish any man alive. In a few minutes he had returned filled with concern for Mickey. He never said what had transpired while he was gone, and I never asked; he took that secret to his grave.

"By that time Mickey's arm had swollen to three times its normal size and I knew he needed medical attention without delay. We drove to a small town, located a few miles from the site of the accident. We found a local doctor and asked for immediate aid. He was an impish little man with a slender mustache and cold, piercing blue eyes. There was a tone of sarcasm in his voice. His tone was almost jeering as he inspected the damaged limb. I knew that if I had ever hated anyone at first sight, this was the man. Mickey's fingers were smashed and because of the swelling the nails had to be removed. Without the comfort of any type of anesthetic the doctor began to simply bend the fingernails straight back and clip them off with a pair of scissors. I became nauseated just watching. When I objected, the doctor said, 'He's a big boy and he'll just have to take it like a man.'

"For the second time in a short span my husband's temper flared. Later, in silence, the doctor set Mickey's arm in two wooden splints and informed us that was all he could do. My hate grew more intense, but the problem at hand was more important. For what seemed like hours we drove, and Mickey's condition steadily grew worse. Finally, we arrived in Aston, Idaho, and hurried to an emergency hospital only to discover that instead of reaching the termination of a problem we were met head-on by more anxiety. The doctors informed us that Mickey's condition had been worsened by the makeshift wooden splints and that the blood circulation had been cut off for too long a period of time and that the early stages of gangrene had begun to appear. With the bandages off, Mickey's tiny arm was a dreadful sight. The swelling had distorted the arm even more hideously than at the accident scene. Now, added to the swelling was the revolting tinge of black, decaying blood. The doctors were kind enough but wasted little time in coming to a decision. Mickey's arm would have to be amputated as soon as possible. After a quick consultation with my husband, it was decided that there would be no amputation. We had raised Mickey this far, and we were well aware of his goals and ambitions, none of which could be accomplished without the use of two good hands. With my heart pounding and my throat dry I informed the doctors that I would rather bury my only son with two arms than have him hate me for a decision to make him a cripple.

"For the next three days Mickey's father and I prayed day and night like we had never prayed before and gave Mickey's arm constant care. We massaged the portion unaffected by the breaks, trying desperately to regain the needed circulation. Slowly, ever so slowly, it began to respond. At a point near exhaustion, when it seemed that it would be impossible to continue, the doctors relented and operated on the arm. For a very long period I sat alone in the darkness of the hospital chapel and thanked my Creator for his blessings.

"I would assume that Mickey's school years were the next most interesting portion of his childhood. Not so much his schoolwork—you know, reading, writing, and arithmetic—but the way in which he manipulated his way around those subjects that were unpleasant to him. He hated spelling! So, in order to not receive failing grades, he would trade assignments for work on the teachers' cars. By the time he was eleven years old he had all the mechanical work he could handle. He loved every minute of it. As he grew in size, he also grew in his aptitudes. It was soon apparent that he loved the automobile. Despite some harassment from his father about getting his schoolwork done, Mickey was, for the most part, on his own to do his work as he saw fit. He constantly used his personality to get his way.

"Another thing, Mickey always had a girlfriend. Even back then he had a real way with the girls. This might have been a carryover from his love for his sister. From the time he was a toddling child on to adulthood, Mickey has always loved and protected Collene. If someone ever gave her a bad time, pity him because Mickey never walked away from a fight. His father used to tell him, 'Mickey, if someone is bigger and meaner than you, don't run, just get something to even the score, anything.' I can't say I agreed with this way of thinking, but that didn't matter too much to Mickey's dad.

"It wasn't long before Mickey began to drive on the street—without his father's knowledge, naturally. And then it was racing on the street and at the dry lakes around the California deserts." With a quick motion of her hand, a motion that I would find to be hereditary from mother to son, she cut off her statement, concluding, "I'm not going to get into the racing side of Mickey's life because I think that is his own personal business. He loves it so, and I have always been proud of his achievements. He knows more about them than I do."

The hour had grown late, and I wondered how much more the aging mother could stand. She looked tired and her eyes had lost some of their glow. I asked her if she would like to terminate our taping session and continue it at a later date. Again, she waved her hand and stated, "We started, so we may as well finish."

For the next hour or two, her voice in a quiescent tone, she rambled about Mickey's childhood: his love for his sister, his early business ventures, his devotion to the automobile, his dependability when his father was away during World War II, and his genuine interest in life. As her voice grew quieter, I suspected that a delightful evening was drawing to a close as my gracious hostess grew tired. Finally, she admitted her fatigue, but there seemed to be something more that she wanted to tell me. By her manner it was apparent that the picture, etched indelibly in her mind, was not a remembrance of thoughts that were pleasant. Her next statements were only an attempt to bring this long-suppressed memory to the surface.

"Mickey was sick for almost a year," was her opening statement. She continued without letting me speak the question poised on the tip of my tongue. "He became

Mickey and Collene with their father, Marion, late 1930s.

listless and the doctors discovered that it was mononucleosis. He almost died, because he had lost the will to live." Obviously, my questions could not be held back forever. I asked what had happened. She hedged. Then she gave me a very evasive answer to my question. "Mickey had a very tragic accident when he was fifteen years old; it changed his entire life." I wanted details, but all I could get were traces. Unwillingly, she continued, "I never saw anything like it. After he was cleared, he just lost interest in the outside world. Then he got sick. After a year and a half, he was better physically, but I believe that from that point on, mentally he was never the same. He became a loner, his moods became more intense. Also, his desire to succeed became stronger."

As I pushed the issue, Mrs. Thompson stood her ground. "Mickey should be the one to talk about this time of his life and I don't believe that it is my place. This horrible incident was the most significant happening in Mickey's young life and I'm not sure that he wants to disclose the details in a book that will be read by thousands of readers."

From that point in our conversation everything suddenly became anticlimactic. Mrs. Thompson sensed the problem and used her motherly intuition to eliminate the situation. "Well, it seems that I have been about as much help as I can be." Her voice had become hoarse and her eyes fatigued. She had given me a beautiful start to a difficult project. Now she had reached the end of her usefulness and instead of slipping away as her age would suggest, she thwarted my questions and sent me to the remainder of the task at hand filled with intrigue and unanswered questions.

As I touched her hand when I left, I knew that here was a story within a story and that I had just been exposed to a person who would influence my thoughts for many years.

GROWING UP TOUGH IN A
HARD WORLD

By our second meeting, Mickey had recovered sufficiently from his back injury to be up and around. His temperament had also changed. He was demanding, filled with energy and full of suggestions about the book. First, he dispensed with formalities and gave me a verbal reprimand for using several curse words in the introduction of the book. It was his wish, from this point forward, that the story be told without the use of abusive language. When I claimed that everyone used a descriptive adjective on occasion, he snapped back that children would be reading this book, that he didn't like bad language in print, and that the story would be just as interesting using some other words. I agreed.

Although his mother had been exceptionally helpful in laying the groundwork for this story, I wanted Mickey to review his childhood somewhat with me. We decided to skip some of the less significant facts and try to continue with those items that were important in the development of his personality.

For an hour or so we sat together, and Mickey rambled slightly as he spoke about his early life. He attended school with a variegated mixture of blacks, Mexicans, and assorted nationalities. "There were only two of us white kids who really got along with everybody because we would fight, play, compete on any level with anyone. For this reason, the kids from minority backgrounds respected us. If they wanted to play, I was ready, but on the other hand if they wanted to fight I was always ready for that too. I presume that my mother has already explained my father's position on that score. If I ever came home and told him that I was beaten in a fight, he would simply give me another beating and send me back for more. It may sound a little uncivilized in thought, but it proved to be quite effective in establishing my foundations for life."

I realized, as we talked, that it was only a matter of time until the automobile would appear in the story. Mickey quickly tired of the trivia of childhood and dismissed it by clearing his throat and beginning a new subject. This was another trait that would repeat itself throughout the entire series of taping sessions. If he didn't want to talk about something, Mickey would change the subject and you would be hard-pressed to extract additional information.

"I bought my first car, a '27 Chevy, at the age of eleven for $7.50 and a model airplane. It was a basket case; I had to carry it home in a wagon piece by piece, but it was all mine and I paid for it with my own money.

Previous page: Marion Lee Thompson Jr. was born in 1928, and his beloved sister Collene was born three and a half years later.

"Money was about the scarcest commodity I knew of at this time, and I was forced to use every conceivable resource at my disposal. In other words, I was kind of a hustler. I sold papers, mowed lawns, worked on my teachers' cars at school, and even shined shoes. The latter profession came to an abrupt halt when my father found me in a barbershop doing 'nigger's work' as he called it. I always felt sorry for my dad and his prejudice toward certain people. But it was the way he was brought up and there was no changing him. It must have been difficult for him at times because two of my closest childhood friends were of minority races. One guy was part Chinese and part black; his name was Guy Quon. The other boy, Alfonso Arenies, was Mexican. These two kids were my constant companions; we played sports together, we went to school together, and we fought together. They taught me a lot about prejudice and racial discrimination. I only wish my father could have felt the warmth and genuine affection we had as friends. To this day, I have no discriminatory feelings about any race. I judge a man on what he can do, what he produces, not on the color of his skin. I think people who do are just plain stupid."

Mickey seemed preoccupied as he related the details of his friendship with these two boys, and he became more immersed in thought as he continued to speak. "You know, those guys really helped me when I was young. I had a paper route, one of several jobs I had, only this paper route was sort of special. There was a section

Thompson, seated center, met his first wife Judy, third from left, while the teenagers were on Easter vacation at Newport Beach, California.

Thompson raced his '36 Ford coupe at El Mirage Dry Lake in the Mojave Desert approximately seventy-five miles northeast of Los Angeles. Hot rodding got its start in the Southern California dry lakes.

of town where the Pacific Electric [a streetcar line that ran through Alhambra and performed much as a railroad would today] kept and housed their section gangs. These 'gangs,' as they were called, were made up solely of Mexican-Americans and they worked laying track and repairing the line. For the most part they lived in substandard housing shacks and sometimes even old outmoded railroad cars, not fit for pigs, let alone humans. The entire area was a ghetto. Strangely enough, though, the people hungered for news and they tried very hard to keep up with what was going on. Consequently, that particular neighborhood was one of the best routes in the city. The only problem was that most of the paper carriers wouldn't go near the place. Papers had to be delivered by 3 or 4 a.m. on Sunday and 6 a.m. during the

Thompson also raced his coupe at Santa Ana Drag Strip when it opened in 1950. He turned a speed of 96 miles per hour at the nation's first commercial drag strip.

week, so there was some hesitation about going into a place like this that early in the morning. It didn't bother me; after all, they were only people. And after they learned that I posed no threat to them, they accepted me. I became their numero-uno paperboy. I feel that much the same set of circumstances is going on right now. Fear and intimation have caused a sense of suspicion among races and everyone strikes out at what he doesn't understand. Maybe if our leaders could deliver papers some morning they would learn a heck of a lot about human nature."

I reached over and shut off the tape recorder and snapped open a can of diet soda pop that always seemed to be in plentiful supply at the Thompson house. Even this early in the story I was beginning to see Mickey Thompson in a different vein than the public image from which I had originally drawn my presumptions. When we continued talking, Mickey resumed that tale of his first car, that old Chevy.

"My dad felt pretty safe in giving his consent for me to have a car at the age of eleven. The vehicle was located less than a mile down the street on which we lived, but for all intents and purposes it might as well have been ten miles away. I had no way of getting it home. The car didn't run, and even if it had I wasn't allowed to drive. After all, my father was a policeman. A juvenile driving a motor vehicle was a breach of the law and my father wouldn't have hesitated for an instant in stopping his own son from breaking the law. But man, I wanted that car!"

That statement, "Man, I wanted that car," was more than just a simple utterance. I noticed that whenever Mickey was really engrossed in making a point, he would invariably accent the statement by pounding his fist into the palm of his hand, looking me in the eye, and say, "Man, I really wanted . . ." and then he would name a particular object. It was a very meaningful gesture and, in most cases, no matter how difficult the task might be, he used every ounce of stamina he had to obtain the object of his desire. That old Chevy was very important to Mickey and the moment that he said he wanted that car, I knew he would have it.

He continued, "For the next nine months or so, I would go down the street with my wagon and remove a part or piece. When a part was too heavy, I would con some of my playmates into helping me. Slowly, ever so slowly, the majority of the car was sneaked into my backyard. As I became aware of the fact that I would eventually get the car home, I became very excited, almost frantic. I pushed, bullied, borrowed, and promised everyone who would listen to me to try and persuade them to help. Finally, the day came when the entire vehicle stood, or rather lay, in a heap in my backyard. I was very happy. I knew as long as the parts and pieces were in my backyard, then I could find a way to put the car together. For endless hours I read every book I could get my hands on to educate myself about the interior workings of my new project. I hounded the shop teachers in school even though I didn't have a shop program at the time. Everyone I asked helped. Even my father softened, and he proved to be one of my favorite teachers. His guidance was stern, but it was also filled with love; not the candy-coated variety, but genuine father and son love, the kind you never have to talk about.

"At the end of one year the '27 Chevy stood ready to run. At this point I had $14 invested. I sold the car for $125 and bought a Model A Ford roadster and from this point on cars were always foremost in my mind."

I couldn't help asking if making a profit was the only reason for his fervor and zeal whenever he began a project. Mickey looked at me in mock wonderment. "No, I loved cars and mechanical things, but I also had a great desire for personal

Thompson's sister Collene with her future husband Gary Campbell. The couple was extremely supportive of Thompson throughout his life.

possessions. Don't get me wrong: I always had three square meals, clothes on my back, and all of the staples. But my folks had only a moderate income and I rarely had anything new as far as a child's tangibles were concerned. Most of my toys were homemade, and the things I enjoyed the most, I had built myself. From this feeling—I guess you could call it insecurity—I developed an insatiable desire for material assets. From the beginnings of my early childhood I had had this drive to become a millionaire. I just couldn't help it; it was just there. This, coupled with my love for machines and a hatred of being bound by the average eight-hour workday, caused me to become what I am today."

For the next hour or so Mickey's conversation engrossed me to the limit of my concentration. His words were so vivid, and the imagined whirl of color and noise prompted me to forget about my reasons for being with him and to relive my own childhood and the powerful elixir that drew young boys toward the automobile. Mickey talked of racing stripped-down Ford roadsters on dry lake beds that have long since become government installations, air force bases, and the like. Anyway, it was different then. I closed my eyes and I could hear the throaty roar of unmuffled engines; it was the beginning of the auto age. I saw suntanned men wearing jeans and T-shirts clustered in groups around surplus World War II airplane wing tanks that had been converted into four-wheeled bullets filled with all of the ingenuity that an untamed mind could conceive. There was sun and dust and the succulent smell of a cool morning combined with a feeling of creation and progress. It was called hot rodding and for those of us who have been exposed to it our lives had been changed in a way that only another soul-suffering auto buff would understand. Today the old dry lakes are gone forever, but from those miles of sand rose heroes who have outlived their own progress.

Mickey seemed to sense the fact that his narrative was falling on the ears of a receptive audience. He excused himself from the couch, a spot he found to be the most comfortable during the long hours of taping, and, removing his pants, climbed into a portable sauna located in the dining room of his apartment. "You know I raced on circle tracks around Southern California when I was just fourteen or fifteen years old." He seemed almost arrogant as he rolled onto his back while cramped inside the sauna.

"I used to build my own engines and even grind my own cams back then. I would go to the tracks and the promotors would want nothing to do with a punk kid. But sometimes they had their backs against a wall because there weren't enough cars to fill the field, so they would let me run—in the back, naturally. I had to tie myself in with rope. We didn't have roll bars and the helmets back then were next to worthless, but it didn't matter to me. I would start last and race as fast and as hard as I could. We would bang wheels and slide around corners, ricocheting off the wooden walls. It didn't take long until I earned a reputation and the promotors began letting me run all the time."

Listening to Mickey I couldn't help feeling sorry for those who had missed that period in motor-racing history. I recalled the nights I had sat huddled behind cyclone fencing watching old roadsters—hot rods, as they were called—sliding around half-mile dirt tracks, tracks that became the testing grounds for some very famous race car drivers. I'll never forget Culver City, the world's fastest quarter-mile. And Carroll Speedway, the half-mile track that saw the diminutive figure of Mickey Rooney, with teeth clinched, arms extended, and head bobbing, as he drove his "hot rod" in the movie *The Big Wheel*. I remembered the nights—it always seemed so much more exciting when the cars raced at night. Maybe it was the eerie cast of the arc lights, the noise, or the fact that you were out at night and that feeling made the whole scene more stimulating. Regardless, watching and smelling and breathing in the exciting vision of those early predecessors to modern-day racing machines was an experience that I for one will never forget. Mickey, I thought, was very lucky to have been able to participate, no matter how illegal or how much like an outlaw it may have made him look. He was very fortunate indeed.

After boiling himself nearly to the consistency of a pot of overcooked pasta, Mickey pulled his reduced frame from the sauna as if the conversation had set his mood and he was climbing out of an old roadster after twisting and turning for fifty laps. He collapsed back on the couch. His eyes became heavy, fatigued by the fact that he was up and in his shop at 6 a.m. every morning. His condition made continuing useless.

Several weeks passed before Mickey and I were able to get together for another taping session. This time his mood had changed completely. He was on the defensive; he scrutinized my every move. He questioned me about the book's progress and then fired a couple of pointed questions about my ability. It all seemed out of character for him. I had never witnessed this side of Mickey Thompson. The side his adversaries saw. He knew that the time had arrived to discuss the one single point that changed his entire life. The incident his mother had hidden and refused to discuss earlier. I tried to convince him that it had to be told, no matter how painful. He disagreed. His procrastination continued for two more meetings. He was too busy. The Baja 500 off-road race had to be run. He didn't have time to meet with me until after the race. Too much to think about. Finish what you have on tape. The excuses went on. A week turned into a month, but finally a date was set.

You could have cut the tension with a knife as I plugged in the tape recorder. Mickey faked a few smiles and I fought back a mild case of fidgetiness. Actually, for myself there was a sense of excitement because I felt that for the first time since the beginning, I was unearthing the true feelings of Mickey Thompson. This wasn't some rehashed press release; this was untapped emotion at the gut level.

Mickey's voice quivered slightly as he began, "There was a man who lived in the neighborhood close by the church my family and I attended. And, as sometimes happens, he had the emotional makeup that attracted the impressionable—namely, the young. His name is of little consequence; the only real, substantial point is that we grew to be friends. He was older, but as you know, because of my interest in the automobile I sought out older men who had the knowledge for which I so desperately searched." Mickey's voice grew even more tense as he spoke. "This man convinced me to join a small organization of young people, something similar to the Indian Guides [an organization for fathers and sons in which the young men are taught manual skills]. He didn't take my natural father's place, it was just that I respected him and liked being around him. We fished together; I brought my inventions and the old cars that I built to him for his observations.

"When I was fifteen years old, I got my beginner's permit and began to drive on the street. I had an old Model A roadster then and used to drive everywhere for any reason. I just couldn't stay out of that car.

"One Saturday night I had skipped church services and had been driving around when I decided to drop by the church just as the congregation was exiting. It was

a beautiful night and a warm breeze ruffled my T-shirt and brought the nearly unmuffled sound of the engine back to my ears. I really loved that old roadster."

Suddenly, I noticed that Mickey's eyes were filled with tears. I felt uncomfortable, my hand instinctively reached for the volume control on my tape recorder. It was a demoralizing effect on your physiological makeup to see another man about to cry. You suddenly realize just how vulnerable human emotion can be. I wanted to change the subject. I was sorry that I had placed so much importance on this situation, but there was no turning back now.

Thompson, fifth from right, and Judy, fourth from left, served as best man and matron of honor at Gary and Collene's 1951 wedding.

Mickey continued, "I saw the people milling around the church as I approached. I also noticed a few figures poised before crossing the street. I lifted my foot from the throttle and blipped the gas as I downshifted into second gear. A split second later my right foot came down on the brake pedal. It went to the floor. There was no time for an evasive move. I pulled back on the steering wheel in a frantic effort to stop the car. It was ridiculous, you can't stop a vehicle by pulling on the steering wheel. A sickening thud followed. And a featureless figure flopped onto the pavement like a discarded sack of laundry."

Mickey stopped speaking for a moment as he tried to collect his thoughts. I didn't utter a sound because here before me was a man reliving a most horror-filled clip of memory film. His eyes were now completely filled with tears. "Tom, I wanted to scream, cry, say I was sorry, run, stay, disappear, relive the final few seconds all at the same time. I wanted desperately for that night to be over. Death is terrible enough, but when you're the instrument you just can't accept reality. The reason the car had not stopped was because a battery cable had wrapped itself around the cable for the mechanical brakes. It would not allow the brakes to work, but that is immaterial now. There was a police investigation and I was cleared, but the first signs of paranoia and melancholia had begun to set in. Despondency was next. I came down with mononucleosis and for almost a year it was a hit-and-miss proposition whether or not I would live. I just didn't care. Slowly, I recovered and regained my interest in the automobile."

As always, when he wished to put an end to something, Mickey brushed his hand over his eyes and said, "Hey, let's continue taping toward the end of the week. I just got to get a few things put together and you're blocking my way." I saw that reliving this most unpleasant experience had drained his mind, and for a moment I wondered about the happy-go-lucky boy and what he would have been like if a few seconds had not cut away the enchantment of youth. From that night on, although the subject of death was discussed on many occasions, the effect would never be the same.

QUARTER-MILE
MAYHEM

As Mickey and I sat down to discuss the time that he spent building the once famous, now demolished Long Beach Drag Strip, I couldn't help but feel that if any one chapter was to hold an identity for the preponderance of readers, this would be it. A large percentage of men between the ages of twenty and forty, who are or have been auto enthusiasts and have lived in the Southern California area, undoubtedly have spent time at this drag strip.

Located on a dismal, featureless piece of landscape surrounded by railroad train yards, bean fields, and oil refineries, Long Beach Drag Strip was not an attractive spot. But, for its purpose, the strip carried a mystique that grew throughout the years. On the cool, fog-shrouded Saturday nights when the races were run, a chemical change came over participants and spectators alike. It was uncanny. There seemed to be an ever-present explosive feeling that hung like the fog and it was as if at any given moment the semiliquid mixture of human emotions and mechanical ingenuity would jell into a spectacular experience. It was partly the Thompson image—its overacting, its hustle and flash—and it was partly the personality of that strip of asphalt that made this a racetrack capable of recording history.

Drag racing as a sport began on the streets of Southern California and as it grew, it moved to legal strips. It was during this incubation period that Long Beach Drag Strip was born. It provided a place for the youth of the day to use their pent-up energy and to express their real love for the automobile.

Because I spent a considerable number of weekends within the confines of Long Beach Drag Strip, writing and reliving its history, it holds a special nostalgia for my mind that has become filled with adult trivia. On that strip I have felt fear, joy, and anxiety. I have seen death. I have seen a friend reach fame in a sport that was shunned by some, and even hated by many. *The Loner*, the first book I wrote, focused exclusively on the sport of drag racing. In it, I discussed in depth the era that existed during the 1950s—an era of change. It is the same time period that we are about to relive.

The automobile had a magnetism hard to define. It lured the young away, out into the street. It made them mobile. A car was status back then; it gave the owner an inroad to the most important thing on every young man's mind—girls. Without a car, girls, prestige, sex, and status among your peers was impossible. A car was everything.

Previous page: Thompson had the luxury of testing during the week at his beloved Lions Drag Strip. Preparing to attack international acceleration records, he built this little dragster powered by a supercharged four-cylinder Tempest (essentially half of a Pontiac V-8).

The so-called "slingshot" dragster was covered with a crude streamlined body including a plexiglass canopy, making it the sport's first fully streamlined dragster.

As Mickey began to speak, I felt a slight twinge of excitement stir. "Long Beach was one of the first drag strips in the country. It also set a precedent as the first commercially built racing facility. Previously, airports were converted into drag strips for Sunday afternoon racing. The whole idea of building a strip was to keep guys from racing in the streets. Back in the early '50s, street racing really became popular and every kid with a set of dual exhaust pipes practiced it. With the absence of rules, street racing was not only looked down upon by adults, but the local police also ran continuous raids on the favorite street-racing haunts. The danger of an accident was ever present. I don't have to tell you what a tragic situation an accident is and what a long-lasting effect it has on your entire life. I killed my best friend!

"There were nine local Lions Clubs in the Long Beach area, and they had put together $5,000 each to try and build a drag strip. Unfortunately, they didn't know a damn thing about running, or building, a drag strip. They were forced to hire me to try and get the job done. Looking back, I think they offered me $75 a week to start. The only reason I took the job was because I wanted to help the guys who wanted to race and to give them a safe place to do it. I sure wasn't planning to get rich. Besides, I had three jobs as it was.

"Once under way, it was obvious that $45,000 wasn't anywhere near the figure needed to finish the project. Realistically, it would take another $65,000 to conclude the project. That didn't bother me, though. I really wanted that strip and like anything else, when I have set a goal to get it, I figured it was a job that had to be done and I was the only one who could complete the task.

"Within a couple of weeks after construction began, money ran short and I approached one of the Lions Club board members. His name was Baker, I believe, and he was a hustler just like myself. Baker saw the potential the strip had, not only in revenue for the charities supported by the Lions Clubs, but also for the more important asset of keeping the streets safe. The details are vague, but Baker didn't make any secret of his feelings. His scheme was simple—to build the strip with whatever raw materials were available. The hell with orthodox practices. And that is exactly what we did.

"After the original money was spent, we began building whatever was needed with nothing more than our bare hands. We scavenged telephone poles from 'Ma Bell,' we cannibalized boiler pipe from the local oil fields to serve as fence posts. When the paving company began paving the strip the money was committed to other interests, so the mention of payment was never brought up. When the job was completed it couldn't be brought up. Tempers flared, but I gave them my word that every dollar owed would

Previous pages: When Lions Associated Drag strip opened for business October 9, 1955, it was as basic as could be. There was just a strip of asphalt and a plywood-covered timing tower. Thompson was the only paid employee and continued to bring new and innovative ideas to the strip for the next eight years.

Below: In 1954, Thompson reasoned that the secret to drag racing success was in gaining any possible traction advantage. He felt that placing the driver behind the rear axle and coupling it directly with the engine-transmission assembly would focus the weight on the rear driving wheels.

be paid. I just charged everything that I couldn't borrow. Word got around quickly and suddenly those vendors involved in building the strip realized that there wasn't any money to pay building costs. But before they could react, I had the strip built. Then I called everyone concerned to a meeting and stated that there was no way anyone was going to get paid unless the strip was allowed to go into operation and if all concerned just settled back, some type of payment plan would be developed."

Mickey laughed as he continued. "Every man who left that room hated me for hustling them, but at the end of two years every one of those concerned was paid in full. To me, that's just good business. Life is made of chances and if you sit back you can never move toward your goals.

Early test runs on the dragster were made at nearby Pomona Drag Strip. The first version of the body was made from cardboard and fabric.

"Once completed, Long Beach Drag Strip instituted many first-time innovations. It introduced the major advances in timing equipment, and we even proposed new concepts for governing events.

"To be honest, the first couple of years of the strip's evolutional development were extremely difficult. The areas in which the strip was located—San Pedro, Wilmington, and Long Beach—were just plain bad neighborhoods. Street gangs were commonplace, and once the strip was in operation it became a place for these gangs to meet. For the most part, gang leaders brought their members to the drag strip, not to race their cars but to prove themselves capable of instigating trouble. Most of the gangs hated authority. It was just the times in which we lived.

"There wasn't a night that went by when I didn't have at least one fistfight, and most of the time there were two or three. I remember walking through the pit area; it was always dark and usually cold, foggy, and lonely. Suddenly, from behind a car or out of the shadows four or five figures would materialize. Sometimes nothing was said; sometimes insults and then fists flew. They punched

Thompson needed a sponsor for his trip to the first NHRA National Drags and convinced William Hannon, right, who managed vast real estate holdings in the San Fernando Valley, including the San Fernando Drag Strip, to have the newly developed Panorama City cover the cost of the trip.

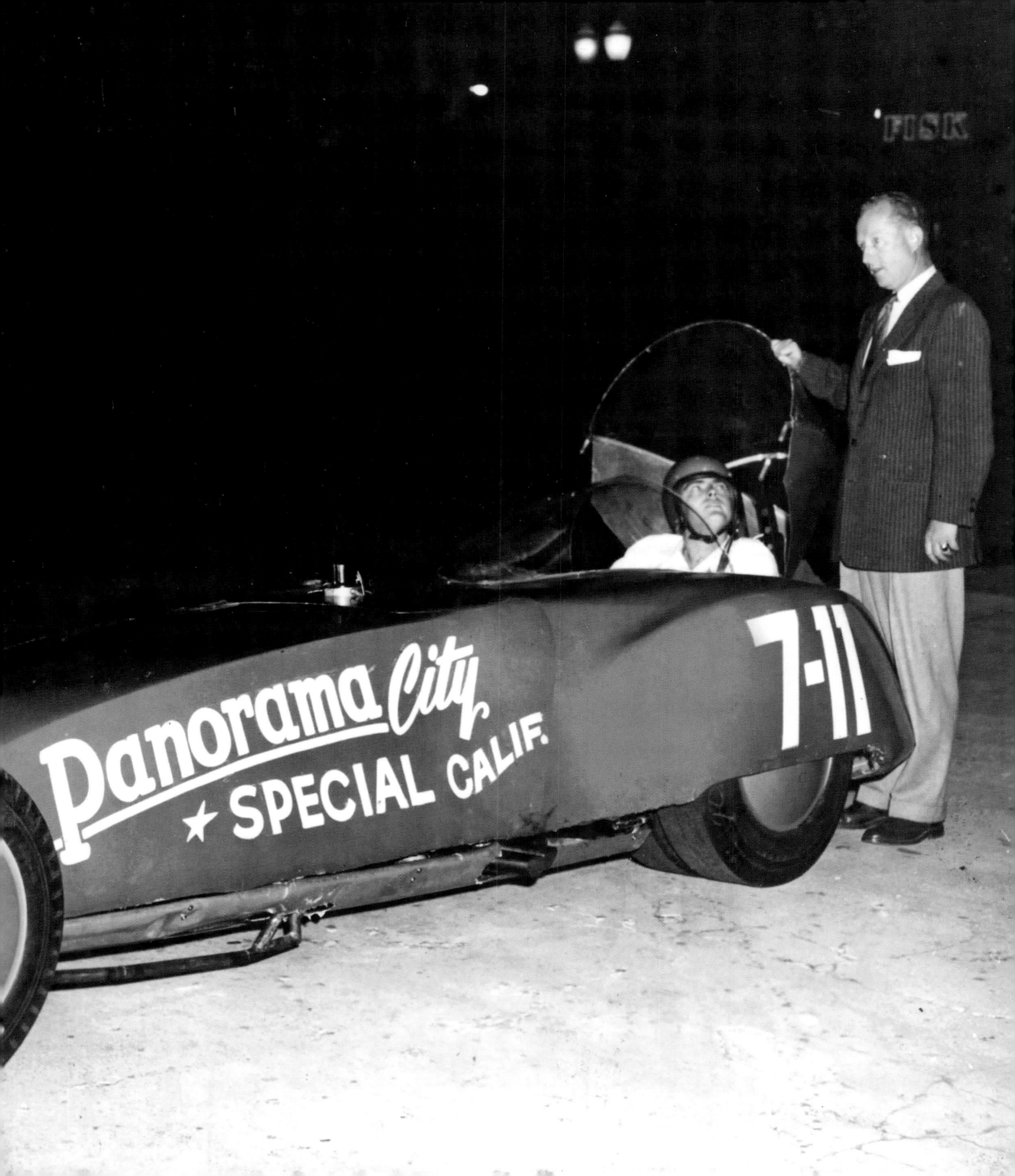
FISK
7-11
Panorama City
★ SPECIAL CALIF.

At the first NHRA Nationals in Great Bend, Kansas, in 1955, Thompson and his slingshot left a lasting impression but fell to the meet's eventual Top Eliminator, Calvin Rice in the far lane.

and kicked me, and I returned the favor. If the opportunity presented a wrench or club, well, that was all the better. My face was always bruised, and fractured knuckles became like so many household nicks. This pressure forced me to become cruel and, in some instances, unreasonable.

"It got so bad that the number of fights grew to four or five a night. Most of the fights were a result of overdrinking. I wouldn't allow any drinking, so I'd see guys sitting in a car drinking beer and when I requested that they give up the beer or leave, they politely told me to go to hell. Well, that was all it took. I remember really punching one guy in the mouth, and blood and teeth flew. It was one of those rare occasions when I won. Anyway, he ended up bent over, half lying against a parked car. He had one hand cupped over his mouth and blood oozed from between his fingers and his words were garbled with hate and pain. The rationalizing behind his words suggested that he would sue me for beating him up. I recall grabbing him by the jacket and looking him coldly in the eyes as I said, 'Look, you son of a bitch, you'll have to get in line.' That's how ruthless you become when violence is a way of life. And let me tell you something, brother," Mickey pointed his finger squarely into my face as he spoke, "that habit of punching first and asking questions later has haunted me all these years since then. I can't count the times when I let my temper run away with my reasoning. Those first few months at Long Beach turned my temper into a hair-trigger form of reaction.

"Nearly a year passed and when we moved racing from Saturday nights to Sunday afternoons, the fighting tapered off slightly. Some type of quiescent feeling had to evolve. I had fought every gang leader in the whole cockeyed area. Also, by this time, drag racing had begun to catch on and more and more guys came down on Sunday to race, and not to fight. Slowly, the machines were becoming more sophisticated. There were even a few dragsters."

In the middle of our taping session, Mickey suddenly stopped talking about how he built the drag strip and began elaborating on the history of early drag racing machines, how he built one of the first dragsters in America, and how he designed the first slingshot dragster (the driver sits behind the rear wheels) in America. I cursed and told him, "Let's stay with the original plan of talking about the strip and its history." My intimidating remarks had no effect on him as he continued to elaborate on his accomplishments. I would just have to reconcile myself to the fact that once something aroused his ego to make a point, the point would be made.

As would happen time and time again throughout the period we spent working together, my sentiments were overwhelmed by the fervency of Thompson's personality. Soon I was once again propelled backward in time.

The pressure of the steel links of the fence caused tiny indentations in my palms. A slight breeze stirred the aroma left by burning rubber, a repulsive smell to some, but to a young boy entranced by sorcery worked right in front of his eyes, odors of identification were all that were absorbed. With sheet metal bodies flapping, tires squealing, and uncapped exhaust pipes screaming, the frightening-looking vehicles poised for an instant at the starting point and then leaped away. They would dart and hop and perform a series of gyrations as an overpowering pair of wrists tried desperately to keep the trajectory straight. Unbelievable speeds were attained by these tiny homemade projectiles—from zero to 150 miles per hour. At the time, these speeds were doubted by experts, who thought the feat to be impossible.

I remembered seeing Mickey Thompson for the first time. His vehicle was completely homegrown. And as with every car he has ever built, and probably will ever construct in the future, it was still being repaired and replenished until

Following pages: Although Thompson jumped into the lead at the start, Rice's J.E. Riley Special was able to make up the deficit, eliminating Thompson from competition.

the very last second before it began its flight. Thompson was everywhere, yelling, commanding, cursing, and laboring harder than all concerned. He would bolt into the car—Levi's and T-shirt for a driving suit—strap on a helmet, and erupt down the narrow ribbon of asphalt with all of the intense, vehement energy his turbulent spirit could exercise. With teeth clenched, he tried every time to outperform all his competitors. With nothing more than sheer courage he finally attained speeds of 150 miles per hour in a scant 1,320 feet.

Not only did Thompson set records with his race cars, but he also slowly began to develop the drag strip at the same time he worked at a car lot and a small garage. He was also instrumental in conceiving what later became a national habit—the drive-in restaurant. Mickey founded one of the first ten-cent hamburger drive-in stands in California. His energy was inexhaustible. As he continued relating these events, it was difficult to visualize this middle-aged, slightly portly businessman, at the moment draped over an expensive couch in a $600-a-month apartment, clad in dirty jeans

The Pan American Road Race sparked an interest in sports cars, so in the mid-'50s, Thompson bought this Cadillac-powered Kurtis Kraft. He did moderately well against "the sporty car yo-yos" until practice for the Riverside Grand Prix in 1957 resulted in a crash and a shattered kneecap.

and an oil-soaked shirt, hair astray. A man people called a rebel upstart, acting as the founding father of one of this country's most exciting motorsports. But it was all true.

"After a year or so, things really began to calm down and a regular weekly racing program was developed," he continued. "There was one governing body for drag racing in the United States—the National Hot Rod Association (NHRA). Wally Parks headed this group and has since then built the organization into what professional drag racing is today. He is a credit to the sport. But, back in the '50s, he was struggling and so was I. There was much discussion about rules and, being the way I am, it didn't take long for the NHRA and my drag strip to have a falling-out.

"I became apprehensive about the fuels [nitromethane and alcohol mixtures] being used by the dragsters. Chassis design and running gear had not kept pace with the speeds. Many drivers were getting injured. Many were burned by the fuel

Still actively drag racing along with his land speed record efforts. Thompson defeated Art Malone in Don Garlits' *Swamp Rat* at the 1960 Bakersfield U.S. Fuel and Gas Championships. Years later he still considered this one of his greatest victories.

from exploding engines. It may sound funny now, but then, 130 miles per hour was far worse than running 230 miles per hour is now. It was terrible. Guys were using recapped tires. There wasn't any protection, or should I say little protection, used around clutch and flywheel components. An exploded clutch and flywheel is more lethal than a mortar shell, and the clutch and flywheel are located between the driver's legs. Need I say more! The exotic fuels being used were the major cause of these malfunctions. Engines could not withstand the tremendous pressures produced with the use of fuel, and subsequently other parts of the cars suffered fatigue.

"After several serious incidents, I decided to ban the use of fuels at my drag strip. All cars, regardless of class, had to use gasoline that could be purchased at a service station. Drivers boycotted the strip immediately, but I held my ground.

Seen in the pits at Great Bend with most of the body off, Ray Brown's fuel-injected Chrysler engine made Thompson one of the first to exceed 150 miles per hour in the quarter-mile.

What the drivers didn't understand was that I had taken it on myself to protect them from themselves. It sounds funny, but drag racers are so competitive and innovative that their major concern is gaining knowledge about space and distance. How to get from a standing start 1,320 feet down a piece of asphalt in the quickest time possible was their total motive. They had no time for protecting their own well-being.

"Most drivers and car builders during this time were dedicated and meticulous craftsmen but they cared little about directing that effort toward safety innovations. Most safety advancements had to be made compulsory before they

Once again at Lions, Thompson worked on one of his Pontiac-powered dragsters based on a chassis from the Dragmaster Company in Carlsbad.

were understood. This is precisely what I had done. Until advances in chassis design and tire compounds could equalize the advances in engine horsepower, those who chose to run my drag strip would have to use nothing but gasoline. At first the NHRA disagreed with my thinking, but soon they too banned fuels. To show their independence, professional racers protested by using aviation gas as a substitute for fuel. They were too daring and would try anything before they would give in.

"There was a drop in speeds because the major ingredient in the formula had been removed. But little time passed before innovation and ingenuity overcame rules and regulations and speeds began to climb once again. This has always been the rule rather than the exception in drag racing. Drivers and builders have continuously been able to overcome all obstacles in achieving higher goals."

For the next few hours Mickey allowed his memories to continue gallivanting through what he called his "drag racing days." He talked about advances in technology, how today's modern, split-second timing systems were developed. He described how a flagman would stand between two vehicles as they poised in defiance, their harsh-sounding, unkempt exhausts brazenly barking, ready for combat. The flagman would crouch, flag behind his back. Suddenly, the starter would leap into the air, waving his flag vigorously as the two machines roared past his leaping frame. Soon, however, sound judgment replaced bravado and the starter was dropped in favor of a "Christmas tree" signal-starting system.

Uproarious laughter broke from Mickey's lips as he talked about old-time finish line procedures. His laugh jarred loose some of my own memories. In those early days, particularly at Long Beach, at the end of the quarter-mile (the distance that became the standard length of a drag race) stood a square tower—a plain, simple wooden tower, with a ladder mounted on one side and a folding chair perched on top of its upper floor. For hours on end a track official would sit, authoritatively calling out which car won each and every race. A problem developed when spotters began calling races in favor of their friends. Many an irate driver discarded a helmet and good manners to climb the tower in an attempt to dismember the originator of a "bad call."

Many moments were on the lighter side during Thompson's career at Long Beach. A major contingent of what now has become the elite core of professional drag racing champions had their humble beginnings at Long Beach Drag Strip. Then they were young, eager, rebellious, and filled with overzealous personalities. Combining these ingredients with the Thompson temper produced a fresh bumper crop of free-for-alls. On one occasion Mickey barred the now-famous Tom McEwen for exercising his mouth. He would not permit "the Mongoose," a nickname McEwen had acquired, to set foot inside the perimeter of the racetrack.

Thompson, left, replaces the aluminum nose piece built by Jim Burrell for the *Assault* dragster.

Finally, relenting somewhat, Thompson allowed McEwen to enter under the stipulation that he must work for the track as an official, not a driver, for a period of six months, free of any payment. McEwen, a stocky, bushy-haired, rather well-off playboy type, accepted the offer, but he continually taunted drivers and officials alike. His practical jokes and cynical remarks were endless.

Despite Thompson's censorship, he had a great rapport with drivers. He remarked that he always ran the strip with a fair hand. He claimed that on several occasions he actually barred his own car, then driven by a man named Jack Chrisman, for rule infractions. Thompson perpetually made a point of fair play and good sportsmanship for all. This trait was then, and continues to be, one of the major aspects of his personality. Although criticized for his mannerisms, Mickey Thompson has always placed "being fair" first in any contest. When I began to assemble the facts necessary to discover what makes this man the way he is, this feeling of "right is right" remained first and foremost in all our conversations, although this trait has been openly disputed by his antagonists. Most people who believe hearsay and know little about Thompson as a person claim that he is a cheat and a liar. I have always found him to be fair. Hard, competitive, and domineering, but fair. In trying to formulate an opinion and substantiate a statement I found his word to be the basis of his personality.

Time flows by like the sweeping second hand of a clock. As the tape continued its rotating movement, Mickey relived his years at the beach. Drag racing grew into a national sport. Weekend events once displaying a larger number of competitors than spectators transformed into jam-packed stands with thousands trying to identify with the masked figures strapped within the confines

During testing at Lions, Thompson shows off the partially streamlined bodywork (the front wheels are still exposed) that would help him break eight international acceleration records as well as six American records.

of weird, bullet-shaped projectiles capable of hurtling down a strip of asphalt racetrack at speeds over 200 miles per hour.

It became commonplace for a dragster, the name used to describe the most sophisticated of the drag machines, to move from a standing start down the length of the quarter-mile racetrack in six seconds. Records were broken as new ideas brought forth higher and higher speeds. And always there was the fierce, unyielding competition of man against man, one brain matching wits with a machine and another human being.

Mickey Thompson was inspired and stimulated by the exhilaration of night after night of competition. He loved the eye-burning caustic bite of the fuel, the malodorous stench of burning rubber, and the speed. Always more speed. Once an event began, it was like an act of love, sensual sensation upon sensation, only the climax of the two

Thompson climbs into his conventional supercharged Pontiac-powered Dragmaster that he raced whenever his busy schedule permitted.

swiftest of all those in competition pitted in a finale brought it all to an end.

After six years Thompson gave up his duties at Long Beach Drag Strip. His record was phenomenal, his reasons for quitting very human. "Every time something went wrong, someone was hurt or killed, friends and families of the victims blamed me. Not always openly, but I felt guilty and empty. And I'm here to tell you now that there were many good men who never saw the sun rise on a Sunday morning.

"You know, there are only so many times your heart can stand the pain of talking to a friend one minute and the next your temples are pounding and fear is knotted in your stomach as you race down the end of the track toward a twisted pile of tubing and aluminum that was once a race car. A strange sickness overcomes you. The figure inside the car is still, except for a last reflex convulsion. There is distortion in the figure—it's a form now, not a human being. The head is slumped, signs of severe injury are everywhere. Sometimes there is blood, other times just a limp body. It got to the point where I was preoccupied by the fear of seeing another person who was close to me end up some Saturday night with a sheet covering him."

As Mickey spoke, some of the events he was reliving became clear in my mind too. On several occasions I was at the drag strip on a night when not everyone that came got to go home when the evening concluded. As gruesome and repugnant as it sounds now, for a long period of time Mickey and I compared experiences about the terror-filled nights we had seen. And it seemed to help. It was a delicate balance— we mourned a few friends and at the same time relived their memory and the good times we had together.

"The death of Leonard Harris was probably the most shocking of all the accidents we had at Long Beach during my years as a manager," Mickey said. As he spoke, a dull gray image slowly began to develop into a living, heart-pounding, full-color replay in my mind. I remembered Leonard's destroyed, twisted race car as it completed its fearsome series of gyrations just a few yards from where I stood. I remember too his lifeless form.

Mickey continued, "Leonard Harris was a national champion dragster driver in the early '60s. He had established a sizable record in a car called *The Albertson Olds Special*. It was an all-out gasoline-burning dragster, powered by an Oldsmobile engine and sponsored, obviously, by a local Los Angeles Oldsmobile dealer. Harris himself was an amazing person. First and foremost, he was an athlete. He had been a gymnast for many years. Although short, Harris was a powerfully built man, with lightning reflexes. His ability to leave the starting line first was the major factor in building his reputation, and he was fast becoming a legend.

"In addition to his attributes Harris was a personable man. His dark complexion, keen eyes, and jet-black hair combined with an ever-present smile to make him popular with the fans. Fellow drivers admired his driving talents as well as his easygoing personality. He was a gentle, popular person but a fierce competitor at the same time. It was this latter trait, his love for competition, that triggered the chain of events that caused the world of drag racing and me a great loss.

For several minutes, with the tape recorder humming aimlessly, Mickey and I reminisced, recalling vibrant recollections long since committed to memory. After a few moments, Mickey grew serious. Again, after some nerve endings had been activated by the stimulation of our conversation, Mickey slumped into the throes of another inauspicious Saturday night. He slapped a heavy hand on the coffee table that rested in front of the sofa on which he sat.

"Mickey Brown, he was a wild kid, but everyone liked him. You remember him, don't you?"

I nodded. I had only seen Mickey Brown race a few times. At the time I was only in my early teens and had just become interested in drag racing. So new was the sport that heroes came and disappeared weekly. Mickey Brown, however, left an impression. I recall that he was extremely aggressive. His mannerisms displayed a kind of abandonment found in those special personalities who capture the imagination by walking the tightrope between recklessness and champion virtue. Mickey Brown was similar in many respects to Thompson himself. He had the ability to turn all attention toward himself and he could, at the same time, convince any skeptic that what he was about to do, right or wrong, was right if he thought it to be right.

"Mickey Brown was one of the wildest drivers I had ever seen. Early in the event, that Saturday night, I told him that I didn't want him driving until he learned some self-control. He had made a run and the car was all over the drag strip.

"I was at the rear portion of the pit area, about a quarter mile from the starting line, when someone came running by to tell me that Mickey was back in the car and heading for the line. I had not discussed my decision with anyone but his crew, so naturally the starting line personnel didn't try to prevent him from running when he approached the starting line. I remember hearing the roar of the engine as his car prepared to make a run. I also remember throwing my hands up in the air in a fit of temper, saying, 'Damn that kid, I told him not to run and I meant it.' As I ran toward the starting line, I heard the car leave in a powerful surge of acceleration. Just about a second elapsed before there was a sudden ring of silence. Then I heard the crowd gasp. It's funny how an entire grandstand filled with spectators will all gasp simultaneously.

"A group of officials and the ambulance crew had already gathered by the time I reached the scene. My lungs were pounding for air and my temper had given way to fear. It was peculiar—the accident did not appear to be serious. He

The fully streamlined *Attempt* shown slowing during record runs at March Air Reserve Base was powered by two different four-cylinder Tempest engines to fit in two different International classes.

only moved about sixty feet down the drag strip before he had gone off the strip. His speed could not have exceeded 50 or 60 miles per hour. But when I reached the side of the car, which had been righted by this time, it was a sickening sight that greeted my stare. Mickey's head had become wedged between the outside of the roll bar and the track surface when the car had flipped over. There was little doubt that he was gone.

"I became unrelenting and downright fanatical about safety equipment from the day of Mickey Brown's death until the day I left the drag strip. Long Beach was going to be a forerunner in the use of safety equipment. We initiated the use of helmets, fire-retardant racing suits, and later fireproof Nomex-type equipment. We were one of the first strips to use face masks. I just didn't want to keep seeing young, eager, and brave men die because the equipment they were using wasn't safe. Cars improved, engines became more powerful and fuels more exotic, and still there were crashes. Each time it cut me a little deeper.

"Despite all our efforts, and I must mention a near-perfect safety record, one Sunday afternoon a very close and personal friend of mine named Dave Gendian was killed.

"It was the time in the development of the fuel dragster when drivers had gone from using steel wheels to the new, space-age magnesium wheels. Some drivers, Dave included, were using both. The only problem was, the lug bolts that held the wheels on the vehicle had to be changed depending on which wheels were used. In this case, Dave had come to the strip with steel wheels and then decided to switch to magnesium. He had neglected, however, to bring the necessary change of lug bolts. I told him straight out that he couldn't run. He got mad and my temper flared. I told him, 'Goddammit, Dave, you aren't going to run and that's that!'

"Dave managed to force a couple of lug bolts onto the wheels and, still mad at me I presume, went up to the starting line and made a run. I couldn't stop him; again, I was someplace else when a friend needed my help. Halfway down the strip a wheel came off and Dave was killed instantly. I could never say that I was sorry, and I knew he must have felt the same.

"About three years after Dave's death I was sitting in an A&W root beer stand in Parker, Arizona, with my mom, my kids, and my first wife [Judy]. Suddenly a middle-aged man wearing western-style clothing and a hat pulled down over his eyes walked out of the shadows and stuck his head inside the open car window. He looked into my eyes and I could barely make out the reflection of his own pale hollow eyes as I stared back. He said, 'Do you know who I am, you son of a bitch?' The fierceness of his statement took me off guard. I just answered no. 'Well, you should, you killed my son.' His voice cracked as a tear was choked off deep in his throat. For the next several seconds I tried in vain to convince the man that I had nothing to do with his son's death—if anything, it had pained me as much as it had him. My efforts were useless. The man went into a fit of uncontrolled rage. Finally, my family in a state of shock, I jerked my car into gear and drove off, leaving unanswered questions stranded on a wave of curses.

"It was the end for me as the manager of Long Beach Drag Strip. Nothing happened immediately; it actually took time. But from that moment in Parker, I knew that it was over. As I mentioned before, every time someone was hurt or killed, I inevitably felt it was my fault.

"By 1960, Long Beach had reached national prominence. It had grossed over half a million dollars for charity. I was getting a fantastic salary, with a percentage of the gate receipts, and my constant fighting with the board of directors had gotten me a much-improved drag strip. Everything seemed to be on the upswing. But for

One of the many Mickey Thompson projects to appear on the cover of *Hot Rod* magazine was this twin supercharged Pontiac-powered four-wheel drive dragster that was nicknamed *The Monster*.

me, it was time to leave. I was ready to attempt the land speed record with my four-engined *Challenger I.* I had my own speed shop in Long Beach, and I was tired of the constant bickering with my supervisors, so I left. The papers claimed sour grapes, bad feelings, and money woes, but the real reason was buried deep inside my soul until now. I just couldn't face the thought of staring down at another limp, lifeless figure being carried away like so much cold beef. I didn't want to face another harrowed, overwrought, hysterical parent cursing my soul because the one he loved with all his heart was gone.

With Thompson's deep alliance with Pontiac, it was only natural that he'd have Pontiac sedans set up for drag racing. This '61 Catalina was driven by Hall of Fame racer Hayden Proffitt.

"Four years after my retirement from Long Beach I became bored with being a successful businessman and decided to return to supervising a drag strip. This one was Fontana Drag Strip, located in the town of Fontana, California, a highly industrial community a few miles east of Lost Angeles. The strip had gone broke, and after a few arguments about my ability to turn it into a moneymaker, I took over the management of the strip. Actually, I bought the option on the property. Within thirteen weeks I had increased the attendance at Fontana from an average of 800 paying customers on a Saturday night to over 13,000. In fact, we were pulling about 30 percent of our crowd from Long Beach. I just wanted to prove a point.

"I became disenchanted with the operation after a time and sold the option to a group of businessmen. That sale ended in a nine-year lawsuit because the men I sold it to didn't know how to run a drag strip and the strip immediately began to lose money. They in turn blamed me for misrepresenting the strip to them. So, for nine years we have been battling, and morally I'm right and legally they have a bag of technicalities. I could have settled for $20,000 eight years ago, but that's not right. I still believe that I'm right, but that belief has cost me over $40,000 to date with no relief in sight. You can believe me, I'm out of the drag strip business. I proved my point."

As always, when there was nothing left to say about a subject, Mickey simply dropped the mic, lay back, and closed his eyes in a display of mock fatigue.

As I packed up the tape and prepared to leave, Mickey was staring out from his tower apartment at the Long Beach harbor. He didn't say goodnight and his wife Trudy ushered me to the door. I knew that we had uprooted feelings that Mickey had wanted to leave dormant. It was that feeling, that sickening feeling, the one he used to get on a Saturday night when the crowd would stop cheering and grow silent.

BENDING RULES AND PUSHING LIMITS

For the racing buff, the spectator, and those who identify with the "greatest spectacle in racing," the Indianapolis Motor Speedway is the zenith of all their expectations. Its wood-framed grandstands, vast parking lots, modern garages, and gleaming tower evoke the nostalgic past and the promise of anxiety for the future. That's Indy, as the speedway is referred to in racing slang. Everything is there, every ingredient to tantalize, infatuate, and capture the waiting mind.

Late May is a period of awakening in Indiana. That which has lain dormant during winter's grip is energized and becomes imbued with life. Even the air takes on a succulent aroma.

Indy is a combination of odors—spicy hot dogs, beer, and at times you can even smell the excitement. Color, too, plays a significant role in this May pageant. When Indy weekend arrives, colors become more vivid and intense, more alive than on any other day of the year. This 500-mile race draws more than 300,000 spectators each year and is the largest single sporting event in the United States.

On the last weekend in May (for many years the Indianapolis 500 was held on the 30th, but due to changes in floating holidays and traffic problems the race date now fluctuates), a section of Indiana bottomland is transformed from an inanimate state into a kaleidoscopic maze of human emotion. It's a sensual phenomenon. Fights are fought; weak hearts give up; overdrinking is commonplace. There is gambling, debates, lovemaking, all within the confines of one curious day of circumstances. All are drawn, like the moth to the flame, to witness men matching skill and courage against the chance of losing it all, with money as the catalyst.

But there is another side of the coin. For the drivers and car owners, Indy is all of those aforementioned scenes, plus much more.

They face not only fantasy, but also reality. Indy can be filled with frustration, anxiety, and thwarted efforts. There is intrigue interwoven with deceit. Owners clamor for sponsor money, money paid for displaying the names of sponsor corporations on the body panels of the race cars and for the use of the names of winning drivers and cars in a variety of advertising campaigns. Drivers flaunt themselves, ego plumage in full array for a chance to drive those cars that are the best prepared and the most obvious bet to win. All of the activity focuses on a single goal: hard, cold cash. There is always talk of glory and of driving fast cars for the masculine bravado, but for those who deal in the calculating light of realism, and that includes most, money is the prime motivator for whatever effort that is put forth.

Previous page: Despite all the racing he had done, Thompson had the look of a wide-eyed rookie when he arrived at Indianapolis Motor Speedway's Gasoline Alley.

Thompson made an exhibition run at Lions Drag Strip prior to the 1962 Indianapolis 500. The 256 cubic inch aluminum Buick V8-powered rear engine machine was unlike anything seen at the Speedway before.

Both driver and owner have common enemies, however—unyielding enemies with no human emotions. These enemies are conscienceless, spiritless, and phlegmatically one-sided. All who compete at Indy must battle time—ruthless and unrelenting—and physics, action versus reaction, a formidable foe. But in the final analysis it is a simple concrete wall that is the most deadly adversary, an inflexible force field that contains and encompasses all who engage in the game. Everyone who enters fears the wall. For fifty-seven years, men and machines have come to Indy for a day of battle, and for many, the day of color and excitement has been their last.

Indy is a contradiction. It is an event organized by mortals, with human frailties and insipidness. Yet, to succeed takes a superhuman effort. Within a façade of color lies the reality of a task with a goal that far exceeds what has been accomplished in the past. Every year men must hyperextend their talents to the limits of endurance in order to attain results. One mistake can cause instant destruction. There are no second chances.

Indy draws like a magnet. It attracts the masquerader and the innovator. It entices both the cowardly and the brave. It offers fuel for the flame that consumes human egos.

By his very nature, Mickey Thompson was drawn to Indy as if it were there for no other reason than to test his own imagination. Indy was a *must*, but Mickey approached the challenge in his usual unorthodox, Irish bullheaded manner. Thompson lived, faced failures, instituted change, and endured every aspect of the Indy character. Had it not been for the face of death reappearing in his life, Mickey might still be standing on the pit wall waving, cursing, pushing, and trying to resolve problems before they manifested themselves.

"I first saw Indy as a part-time, underpaid pit crew man for a fellow named Ray Crawford. Crawford was a wealthy supermarket owner in El Monte, California, and he participated in a wide variety of racing endeavors, everything from hydroplane racing boats and dirt track cars to stock car racing in the Panamericana road race in Mexico to Indy. However, working in the pits as a crew member leaves precious few moments to enjoy your surroundings. It was just an indoctrination period.

"My head was filled with aspirations after the race. I wanted to come back and run Indy with my own car. At the time this was a ridiculous idea, though. I can't quite remember the exact year, maybe '56 or '57, but anyhow I didn't have any money and I was three or four years from breaking the land speed record. But despite the lack of funds, I couldn't help but feel that someday I would race there. Of course, it would have to be my own way.

"One very obvious fact stuck in my mind that first time: everyone raced the same type of car. Most had roadster-style cars, with front-mounted engines, built first by a famous builder named [Frank] Kurtis, then by a man named A. J. Watson. If they weren't Watson-built cars, then they were cars stolen from Watson ideas. It was a trend, and the cars were successful, so everyone followed.

"Tires were another area that I gave a great deal of thought to. Only one company built tires for Indy—Firestone—and at this time they had almost complete control. In fact, Firestone could lay claim to having all thirty-three cars in the field using their products. This was the state of things year after year. In my mind I felt there was a better way. The tires used were narrow, made from a hard compound of rubber, and extremely tall. In other words, there was a large distance from the track surface, where the tire made contact, to the top of the tire. Too much, in my opinion. Also, it was commonplace for crews to run as much as 50 psi of nitrogen in the tires. When I suggested building a tire that was low profile, squatty, and soft, with the tread across the entire tire and run with a low percentage of air pressure, everyone laughed!

Thompson pioneered smaller wheels and low-profile tires at Indy. Though the tires were first made by Firestone, Thompson later teamed with Sears Allstate to build them with his own M/T brand.

"As far as engines went, most competitors used the workhorse of the speedway, the Meyer and Drake Offenhauser racing engine. There were several deviations, and the most publicized was the Novi, a V-8 monster that had challenged the Offenhauser for years without triumph. I guess what I'm really trying to say is, I figured that there had to be a better way. And I also concluded that within a very short time I would get the necessary money and build a car the way it should be built.

"On paper the rear-engined approach was the only logical way to get horsepower transmitted to the ground effectively. With the engine weight over a pair of driving axles, traction would have to improve. Combine a low-profile chassis with lightweight construction procedures and wider, softer tires and a quicker, faster, more agile vehicle would emerge. However, the establishment considered ideas of this nature the ravings of a fool and a good basis for ridicule. So, for my own protection during this period, I kept most of my ideas tucked away, displayed only on drawing boards inside my mind. It doesn't bother me now, but back then when I was a hot-tempered kid, to be a figure for sardonic snickers made me bitter.

"It wasn't until 1962 that my financial stature and public notoriety allowed me an opportunity to build my kind of car for Indy. I had broken the land speed record and sponsors were clamoring for my ideas. No, I don't mean that, what I really mean is I could finally get some moneymen to listen to my ideas.

Thompson hired long-time hot rodder and sports car driver Chuck Daigh to test-drive his entry at the Speedway. Thompson's eventual driver Dan Gurney can be seen standing in the striped shirt.

"Indy for me started out the same as all of the other projects I had ever been involved with—work began before the money was available! My fervor ignited and I began a race within a race. Jack Brabham, a Grand Prix driver and race car builder, had constructed a rear-engined car for the 1961 Indy. The difference between the two cars, his and mine, was the fact that his car was extremely light and would run a small 1.5-liter engine. In contrast, I wanted to use an American stock-block engine. Brabham had stood Indy on its ear and I wanted to be next. My plan was to build a rear-engined car using a chassis of my own design and a hot-rod engine. What I mean by that is a relief from the standard Offy engine used at Indy—an American passenger car engine. I chose the small-block aluminum Buick, the same basic block used in the compact Buick family sedan. Of course, the engines were highly modified and used fuel injection and racing fuel, the same as the rest of the engines that ran at Indy.

"Anyway, with the help of the Harvey Aluminum Company, my sponsor, we fielded two cars. We had designed and built practically every piece of those cars by hand—all of the chassis work, all of the internal engine parts—and if I do say so myself, they were fantastic for their time. Obviously, being new and untested, there were few who agreed with me. But certain points became undeniable facts. The Harvey Aluminum cars were lighter, were more aerodynamically stable, and provided better traction in cornering situations than the conventional roadsters. However, my expressions of joy became short-lived.

"Once at the track, I created a fervor at the inspection line. To say that the officials in charge of technical inspection gave us a bad time would be the understatement of the century. They had become dreary in the monotony of their job. All of the cars, for years, had remained virtually unchanged in design. Most of the rules were directed toward those vehicles that were in the majority, namely front-engined roadsters. The officials caught one glimpse of a rear-engined car, with an extremely low profile and using a hot-rod engine for power, and it produced utter skepticism. I suddenly became another foreigner trying to pry open the very foundation of the cartel they had built around Indy. When their shortcomings were exposed—the fact that they couldn't even measure the cubic-inch displacement of the Buick engine—indignation turned into harassment. I was so frustrated by the treatment I received that I was sorely tempted to pack up and leave. But finally, the car was allowed to run.

"It was at this point that my troubles really began. Who was going to drive an untested car that everyone laughed at? Only drivers who were so far unable to get rides in other competitive vehicles. To add injury to insult, my pit crew was compiled from the ranks of California hot-rodders. The only non-hot-rodder was a race car designer and engine builder from England named John Crosthwaite. Many of his ideas had gone into actually building the Indy cars and without him and Fritz Voigt we would have never made it.

"As a feeling of despondency erupted within me, I discovered Masten Gregory to drive the number one car. Masten was, and still is for that matter [Gregory died in 1985], one of the most outrageous personalities in motor racing. He is intense. He spoke with a sepulchral, baritone voice that gave his listener the illusion that he was hearing words from the Holy Scripture rather than laments directed at an ill-handling race car. His eyes were hidden by thick, horn-rimmed glasses; his face was gentle but rarely broke from its almost permanent state of *complaisance.*

"Masten's career on the Grand Prix circuit has run the gamut. On a good day, he could run with the most competitive man on the course. But other times he would lose his concentration and become a back marker. He had amassed a substantial cocktail party repartee of sports car experiences, running Le Mans, Sebring, and the Riverside Grand Prix.

"Although born in the United States, Masten lived in Paris, France. Not only did this add to his mystique but also in Europe his greatest claim to fame—that of jumping out of his race car when a crash was unavoidable—was looked upon as just an idiosyncrasy. At Indy, it was a joke!

"To fill the vacant seat of my second car I began going from garage to garage looking for talent. Finally, I crossed paths with Dan Gurney. Gurney, the son of an opera singer, was raised in Riverside, California. He was a hot-rodder and sports car racer, and he and I spoke the same basic language.

"His features were large; he was tall for a race driver, well over six feet, with broad shoulders and a lanky walk. His personality was quiet, sheltering a subtle sense of humor. He was completely dedicated to becoming a world champion driver and a rich businessman.

"At the time of our meeting, Gurney was driving for Porsche in the Formula One European Grand Prix races and was trying to qualify at the 500 in a front-engined roadster that was terribly outclassed and down on horsepower. He had also tried unsuccessfully to run one of the very first turbine cars at the Speedway.

"I convinced Gurney that he should try the rear-engined car I had open, if for no other reason than that the design was similar to that of a Formula One machine. He agreed and only several laps of practice later began to run faster than most of the front-engined cars. Some of the laughing stopped. However, we were still hampered by mechanical problems. And despite all of the advantages of the aerodynamics, our cars were forced to run those obsolete, passé, 16-inch, hard rubber tires. I hated their design. There had to be a better way; I kept pounding that thought into my mind

to force an answer. A lower profile, wider tread with softer rubber was the solution. Time became an enemy and we had to settle for Dan's qualifying time. Looking back, his performance was next to inconceivable. He had taken a car that up to this point had been a laughingstock and qualified it among the top ten. We were about to prove a point.

"On race day, although our problems continued, the overpowering emotional impact of the proceedings made everything but starting second in importance. We were in the field and wanted to win."

Mickey stopped recording for a second, and as he always did when he wanted to press a point, aimed a finger skyward and squinted his eyes. "I want you to believe," he said. "We had a chance to win that race on the very first try.

"Dan was running toward the front from the time the flag dropped. It was a beautiful sight; all of the old roadsters with their deep guttural roar and suddenly our rear-engined Buick would come up, its exhaust pipes playing a steady, high-pitched rhythmical whine.

"Within thirty laps or so, our ace in the hole began to pay off. All of the Offy-powered cars were forced to take on fuel because of their voracious appetites. But the small size of the Buick engine allowed it to run ever so slightly longer before the fuel supply had to be replenished. With fingers crossed, we prayed that if we continued to run as hard as we were and the fuel stops remained in sequence, then some time during the race we would lead. From there on it would be up to the driving skills of Dan Gurney. I really wanted to win that race.

"But my spirits were shattered shortly after the second pit stop. Dan pulled in for fuel and as he began his exit from the pit area the engine died. Our crew worked with fanatical abandon to restart the car. In their haste, the starter motor shaft ruptured a 50-cent seal in the rear end and within several laps precious lubricating oil flowed onto the racetrack and heat caused the rear end to expire and with it our dreams of winning on the first try.

"In 1963 I was filled with confidence. I had not been this excited and had not carried such a keen sense of fascination in a project since the land speed record runs with the *Challenger*. For '63 we built five cars. Actually, we had rebuilt two of the '62 cars and created three entirely new vehicles.

"When we arrived for practice, my ardency quickly turned to anger and frustration. It was the same old story. The cars were too advanced. I had wings mounted on the rear portion of the cars along with a dive-plane effect on the front. These innovations were very similar to the cars they are running today. Anyway, the officials were not equipped to cope with change, so rather than change the rules they simply forced me to remove the wings. This alteration affected a serious modulation in the car's handling characteristics. But removing the wings was only a stepping-stone to the real obstacles.

"Prior to the '63 race I had made up my mind that the tires used at the Speedway were obviously extinct for the type of race car that was going to evolve. With the help of Gene McMannis, a brilliant tire design engineer and now my partner in MaxTrak, a high-performance tire company that I own, I tried to work out a solution. Our problem was to persuade the Firestone Tire and Rubber Company engineers to build a tire to our specifications. In fact, we were so sure of our convictions that we had designed the cars to use a low-profile tire and we had also cast and machined alloy wheels for the tires we expected to build. Firestone said the task was impossible and our calculations were erroneous. I was furious. Armed with our figures, I just fought and cursed until I simply inundated the Firestone engineering staff. Our computations proved correct. Firestone built a tire to Gene's and my own specifications, which was low in profile, wide in tread, and soft in compound or texture.

Thompson confers with driver Dan Gurney during a practice session. Gurney liked the look of the car and was intrigued by the modified Buick engine.

"I had a total of five cars, and we had dropped the Buick engines in favor of hand-built magnesium and aluminum Chevy engines. Three of the cars, including my rebuilt '62 cars, were equipped with 15-inch wheels, and the other two, with brand-new titanium bodies and chassis, were riding on very small, never before heard of 12-inch wheels. Unknown to most of the people at Indy, and especially the drivers, I had tested the cars at the Firestone proving grounds and I was convinced that the new design would work.

"When the Motor Speedway opened for practice it was obvious that the mini-wheels would bear the brunt of the year's verbal abuse. Behind my back, car builders and drivers called them 'roller skate wheels.' What was to prove so ironic and what is still annoying is that all of the innovations—wings; dive planes; low-profile cars; wide, soft, low-profile tires—are exactly the type of equipment being used at Indy today. Many of the new Formula cars express the very shape that my cars had ten years ago. What was laughed at then is now an accepted fact.

"The drivers were also a continuing headache. Any driver who thought he would damage his reputation with the establishment or miss a chance to drive for a big-name team wouldn't touch any of my cars with a ten-foot pole. Professional racing is cruel, and I had to accept drivers who were not in favor. Not particularly because they were not qualified drivers, but for the most part because they were too old, not experienced at Indy, or maybe they just hadn't been winning many races. For some reason they were taboo with Indy's "in crowd." I have always enjoyed seeing rejected personalities find themselves. To me, my drivers were beautiful people.

"Masten Gregory returned with me for the second year as my number-one driver. I added Bill Krause, a young California sports car racer; Bill Cheesbourg, a hulking, cigar-smoking veteran of five Indy races plus years on the oval track circuit around the country; and fifty-one-year-old Duane Carter, who had driven just about every kind of race car there was. He might have been old, but he was a warhorse who really knew his way around.

"When we had tested one of the small-wheeled cars at Riverside Raceway in California, I had flown Graham Hill over from England to help evaluate the car. The new design resembled that of the cars run on the Grand Prix circuit, and it was only logical that we should have the opinion of a driver who had spent a portion of his time driving cars with rear-mounted engines. After testing one of the cars, he had agreed to come to Indy and try to qualify for the race.

"Graham Hill is a story in himself. He is everything an Englishman should be—mustache, slight, well groomed, black hair rather long and combed back, and a dry sense of humor that would ignite like a keg of gunpowder with a minimum of stimulation.

"Graham was a late-blooming star as a driver. He did not even begin driving any type of motorcar until his twenty-fourth birthday. He graduated quickly from a 1934 Morris 8 Tourer to open-wheeled race cars. He tried his hand at motorcycle racing but returned to cars. From that point on he proved to be an aggressive talent. He drove racing cars all over the world. After he left my service, he went on to win the Indy 500 in 1966 and he had already become World Champion in 1962. Aside from Dan Gurney, Graham was the most famous driver who ever drove for me."

Nearly a week passed before Mickey's schedule permitted us to resume taping the chronicle surrounding Indy. Mickey's mood had completed one of its turnabouts, and it was now one of frigid politeness. Facts related to the concluding two years at Indy were unpleasant I was soon to discover, and I now knew Mickey well enough to adjust to the fact than once an unpalatable subject aged in his mind for any length of time he became indifferent and abusive when recalling those events. When disturbed, Mickey could be one of the most apathetic, callous men I have ever met. He spent endless minutes tending to unimportant incidentals before he picked up the microphone. As he spoke, an accusing finger was directed toward me as if I stood in front of him as one his criticizers.

"After just a few days of practice, not the usual weeks it takes to start to put together the right combination to cut fast and competitive laps, my drivers, especially Masten, were closing in on the lap record. It was the tires, obviously. Their design enabled my drivers to move through the corners with more traction, thereby giving them a tremendous advantage. Most of the cars at Indy are capable of running extremely fast on the straightaway sections of the racetrack, but it is only the cars that are capable of negotiating corners with the least amount of speed reduction that are the vehicles proficient enough to win the race.

"As it stood, the United States Auto Club (USAC) officials had forced me to remove the wings and dive planes that I knew would work and had laughed at my wheel and tire design. But now I was proving myself. Tom, I'm telling you, we were ten years ahead of our time with those cars, and if you look at the race cars running today you can see that they are using all of the innovations we had back then.

"Suddenly the tires we had designed and Firestone had built became the most significant items of the year. Once the drivers realized that the times were turning for real, reaction was not long in coming.

"For the first time in Indy history, race car drivers went out on strike. Not for a boost in prize money like the story carried by the news services, but because they couldn't get the tires we had. They thought that the reason we were going faster than most of the field was due to the fact that the tires were of a low-profile, wide design. This was true to a point. However, the drivers had no idea, at the time, that the real reason was the soft

compound of the rubber and the fact that we had elected to run only 30 to 32 pounds of air pressure and not the proven 50 pounds that everyone else was running.

"Firestone became transfixed in a quagmire of their own making. They had made a verbal commitment to pay me $25,000 in sponsor money if the tires we had designed—and they had laughed at—would work. On the other hand, Firestone had supplied their contract drivers with old-style tires on the presumption that there was no way a low-profile tire would be functional. Now the fact was clear that our tires worked, and race drivers, being of the nature they are, refused to race against anyone who might have a slight advantage.

"Several days after the controversy broke out, Firestone tire technicians inexplicably picked up all of the wheels for both my '62 cars and the 'skate' wheels on the new '63 cars and mounted fresh rubber on them.

"Practice resumed and my drivers started to run hard only to begin a mysterious series of spins. Masten smacked the wall. Graham Hill, who had been a little late in arriving, became so frustrated that he wanted to pack up and go back to England. I was completely stymied. The tires looked the same. Finally, we discovered what had happened. Firestone had taken our wheels and mounted low-profile tires of the same compound that all of the protesting drivers were using, not the soft texture our earlier tires had been. They were ensnared in their own transparent code of ethics. It was impossible for Firestone to build and supply tires of our style to all of the other cars because we were the only team with small 15-inch and 13-inch wheels. I had had to buy my own foundry to cast them special. So, to satisfy the cries of protest, we were given a switch. To compound this travesty, Firestone refused to pay me the $25,000 they had promised if the tires worked, stating it was a verbal contract and the tires we had designed were not used in the race."

At that instant Mickey beat a nearby coffee table with his fist, venting some of the frustration that still remained after eleven years.

"Tom, I want this printed! They flat-out lied to me. I was so goddamn mad that from that point on the entire '63 effort began to fall to pieces. Drivers gave up. I hired one of the oldest drivers at Indy, a balding, rough-talking dirt track and Indy veteran named Al Miller. Miller qualified one of the cars so close to the pole position record that no one could believe it. It was the only real highlight left to me.

"During the race, our 500 miles were a succession of traumas. After working on one of the cars for over an hour, right out on the pit apron, much to the dislike of the USAC officials, we finished ninth and thirteenth, respectively. The officials could find nothing in the rules forbidding our working on the pit apron for such a long period of time and that was the only reason they did not attempt to disqualify the cars. Our mutual dislike for each other was kindled further, however.

Previous pages: Rookie Dan Gurney qualified eighth in a field of over sixty entries. A failed grease seal in the rear end concluded the effort for the year. In his first year at Indy, Thompson was awarded the prestigious D-A Mechanical Achievement Award that to him was more precious than winning the race.

"Parnelli Jones won the race in a highly controversial finish. Jimmy Clark, who followed Jones for second place, complained bitterly that Jones had been leaking oil and should have been black-flagged. USAC officials turned a deaf ear and Clark, being the true gentlemen that he was, withdrew the protest. However, Clark had also driven a rear-engined car, a Lotus Ford built by Colin Chapman, and it was clear that the rear-engined configuration was here to stay."

Mickey seemed uncertain as to how he should proceed, then asked if we could pause for a footnote. He began to speak about his feelings for Jimmy Clark. This would mark one of the rare occasions when Mickey deliberately chose to relive moments in his life where the remarks did not totally involve himself. It was rare—however, it would not be the last time. I had begun the deliberate task of breaking down the barrier behind which Mickey concealed his inner feelings. He became very serious as he spoke.

"Before we go on, I want to relate some of my feelings about Jimmy Clark. That's the right phrase, isn't it? Relate."

There was some awkwardness as Mickey's coarse personality dissolved.

"This will probably be the only place in the book appropriate to do so. Most auto enthusiasts and magazine writers knew Jimmy as the World Champion racing car driver. He won every Grand Prix in sight. He drove for Lotus; he won Indy; and he was killed in a Formula Two race at Hockenheim, Germany. What most don't realize was that aside from being a World Champion, and possibly the greatest Grand Prix driver that ever lived, he was a wonderful, warm human being. I spent weeks with Jim in Europe when I followed the Grand Prix circuit closely for a period of time. Jim impressed me so much with his simple, straightforward manner and his psychology of life. He stood head and shoulders above most of the men who have crossed my path in this life. He was sensitive to people's wants and he would share anything he had with a friend. I just wanted to have it down on paper, for all time, that I think Jim Clark was a credit to humanity."

Abruptly, Mickey put down the mic and made an excuse to end the taping session.

Mickey Thompson's Indy effort has been hashed and rehashed over and over. There are many opinions, and books have been written about the events of 1964. I will not take sides, and the opinions of those who have written in the press over the years are theirs alone. The remarks in this story come directly from Mickey and are his memories of the events.

Gathering information about Indy had dragged on for nearly a month! Mickey had business commitments and, at one point, took a few days to recover from a hard spill taken while he was motorcycle riding in the California desert.

On our final session, the mood was perceivably sober. We were both fully aware of what we were about to discuss. Death would reappear in our story. This time, however, I felt a sensitive awareness toward the events about to unfold. Although only by coincidence, I had been acquainted with those involved. And, while separated by 3,000 miles during its enactment, I felt the shock, sickness, and dismay of the tragic event. Mickey's voice was subdued and showed signs of restraint.

"The USAC officials wasted little time in engaging in some political infighting with Henry Ford prior to the 1964 Indy race. Ford Motor Company had developed a powerful new overhead cam V-8 racing engine especially bred for the Indy classic. Its development had cost millions; Ford wanted to win at all costs. Caution aside, they had sent me five of the engines as an inducement to become part of the program. Other teams received the same favor, including Jim Clark, Graham Hill, Dan Gurney, and the Lotus team. But the new engine evolved with some severe drawbacks. It had terminal oiling problems and produced its greatest efficiency only on gasoline. Ford Motor Company advised car owners running the engine to use only standard high-test [racing] gasoline for the race and not the previously used blend of methanol [alcohol] racing fuel, thus setting a precedent for the Speedway.

"Because of the unstable and volatile nature of high-octane ethyl gasoline, I opposed this move emphatically! My fight to stop the use of gasoline was

For the 1963 Indianapolis 500, Thompson introduced the extremely wide low-profile tires that—despite protests—became the norm at the Speedway. Chief Mechanic Fritz Voigt shows one of Thompson's so-called "roller skates" to NHRA officials Jack Hart, Wally Parks, and Ed Eaton in Gasoline Alley.

short-lived because USAC officials had approached my flank and I was forced to consolidate my energies.

"The two cars we had built for the race were highly sophisticated, with great emphasis on aerodynamics. This was a subject the officials at Indy were unfamiliar with. Both cars were extremely low, with 12-inch wheels, wide Sears Allstate tires (I had dropped Firestone or vice versa, so Gene McMannis and I had designed a tire that Sears had built). All of the tires were covered with body panels to give the vehicle less resistance to air pressure. We had also added wings, both front and rear, which were used as foils and air brakes. All in all, the cars were far ahead of their time.

"My wings were banned, and the 12-inch wheels and tires were banned. By removing the wings and small wheels [and tires], the geometry of the car's design was altered. Fifteen-inch wheels and tires were installed. The body panels covering the wheels and tires were modified and in general the cars handled poorly by comparison to the original concept. My drivers, Masten Gregory and Dave MacDonald, had to learn the cars' characteristics anew. Gregory continued having mental lapses, but MacDonald overcame the difficulties enough to run very close to the track record and to scare me senseless on several occasions. He would come charging down the front straightaway with one of the front tires completely off the ground.

"Dave MacDonald was a California road racer who had so impressed me when I saw him run that I immediately signed him to drive for me at Indy. He was young, carefree, with little feeling for responsibility except for his family and driving race cars. He was absolutely fearless, and he was the most naturally talented driver I had ever seen.

"As practice continued, Dave overcame his car's ill-handling temperament and began to run lap times with the leaders. However, a prior commitment back in California forced Dave to leave Indy for nearly a week. This left a lot of problems unsolved. Substituting for Dave during his absence was an old Indy veteran named Eddie Johnson. Johnson had not been too successful at the Speedway, notably because he could not get first-line cars. But he was brimming with experience. Using his talent and his unending courage, Johnson sorted out Dave's car and had it ready for his return. Dave qualified the car toward the front of the field—I can't remember exactly, maybe eleventh or twelfth. Masten cut three fantastic laps on his four qualifying laps, then lost his concentration on the last lap and blew the whole thing. He landed far back in the field. I couldn't get mad; Masten tried so terribly hard.

"On race morning I felt confident, we had beaten the establishment again and put the cars in the field. I knew I was disliked by some USAC officials and some drivers, but on that morning I could have cared less. As the moments before the start grew close, Dave felt his mind was set. He was going to charge from the rear of the pack and get to within striking distance of the leaders as quickly as possible. I reminded him that the race was 500 miles long. He laughed and said, 'I flat got this race backed up and won, I'll be leading this thing by the second or third lap.'

"As the cars came down for the start, a deafening pitch overcame reality. There was color and motion splashing everywhere. All eyes strained as the cars accelerated for turn one.

"On his final carburetion test, run the day before the race with a full load of fuel, Dave had run laps two miles per hour faster than the pole sitter. He wouldn't believe the times at first. So, we knew the car would run.

"By the conclusion of the first lap, as the leaders flashed by, Dave had passed five or six cars. He could run anywhere on the track there was an opening.

"Lap two was just beginning and Dave went low going into turn three, passed a couple of cars, and headed for turn four. Out of four, about six miles per hour faster than the cars preceding him, Dave headed for the main straightaway.

"For an instant before the cars took the green flag, I had a cold, wet premonition something terrible might transpire. But it was only a flash and I dispensed it as prerace nerves. "No omen could have prepared me for the holocaust about to unfold before my eyes."

Mickey's voice grew suddenly subdued and he had to clear his throat before he continued.

"As Dave started down the front straightaway, a slower car moved into his path [the driver involved was later killed in another accident, so I think it only proper to let his name rest in peace], and Dave was forced to slow the car down and try and steer for a clear path. There was no time. The car spun and hit the inside retaining wall, rupturing the fuel bladder [this was one of the first fuel cells used at the Speedway]. Unfortunately, the bladder was filled to capacity and could not stand the force of the blow. The car exploded in flames. In an instant, Dave came out of the flames and I could see him looking around and steering the car. He was alive and conscious; most of the gasoline had been blown clear of the car and for an instant a ray of hope glistened. It was all for naught. Eddie Sachs hit Dave directly in the center of the cockpit as Dave's car slid across the track. Eddie's fuel tanks ignited, and the explosion was too much to imagine. Hysteria broke out, cars careened in every direction. Brave men cried, drivers fought for their lives, and two men died before thousands of unwanting witnesses. I couldn't look. It was the worst crash in Indy history. Fire is the most terrifying way a man can die.

"My first wife, Judy, was sitting with Dave's wife and she tried in vain to console her. Out of pure reflex and frustration I ran full speed toward the field hospital, abandoning the crew, the cars, and our efforts.

"Dave was burned and broken hideously. He lived for only a short time, then gave up. Sachs, a highly emotional, well-liked driver once known as the 'Crown Prince' of the Speedway, died instantly when the car's steering column pierced his chest.

"The aftermath was predictable. We were accused of having 100 gallons of gasoline in the car, which was ridiculous. I swear there were only 46.2 gallons and no more. Dave was blamed for overdriving. Dave MacDonald was a talented driver—he wasn't overdriving, he was racing. Goddamn man, that's what he was!

"It's been ten years since that day. I think about Dave sometimes, but it's never about the race. I see him in his most relaxed moods: holding his kids, kissing his wife, laughing and clowning with the crew. Never tense, with goggles fixed in position, eyes stark, a helmet covering his thoughts as he waited for the engine to bark into life. Never like that.

"I lost complete interest in Indy after '64. Although I ran cars there for the next couple of years it was more or less to try a few new theories, like a front-wheel-drive car I experimented with, and to fulfill sponsor commitments. After several years I dropped Indy completely. I went back every year for a time, but only as a spectator."

Mickey laid the mic down and as always broke off our session with a quick capitulation. "There is nothing more worth talking about as far as Indy is concerned."

Several weeks later, as I put the finishing touches on this chapter, I stared at a photo in *Life* magazine depicting that infamous scene at Indy. There was Dave, firemen spraying his body with foam in a pitiful display of helplessness. It jarred me into the reality that I had once shook that hand lying limp in the picture. I had heard the voice now silent. I was now aware that this story was not just words on paper but a record of real lives. Lives as real as those who would read these words.

Though Thompson never actually raced one of his designs at Indy, it didn't stop him from getting behind the wheel for test sessions. The new No. 82 with its 12-inch diameter wheels was wrecked in practice, but veteran Duane Carter drove its twin to a fifteenth place finish with a blown engine.

CHAPTER 5

FAST TIMES AT BONNEVILLE

To stand in the middle of the Bonneville Salt Flats is an eerie feeling. The Flats cover 3,000 square miles and are absolutely flat and barren. Nothing grows; little lives. They are unforgiving and for someone who has never had the sensation of standing in emptiness, words fall short of explaining.

The first time I stood alone at the Flats I let my imagination run rampant for several minutes and strange images filled my mind. At first I heard the dull creaking and hushed clop of a team of mules struggling to transport a crudely built covered wagon. I imagined three figures huddled together, a man and a woman holding a small child, as they tried to cross the wasteland that I now stood upon. They could not speak, their tongues so swollen from thirst that words were unable to come forth. Like the ill-fated Donner Party of 1846, this family had gambled their lives against an impossible 90 miles of white nothingness. Soon the blinding sun, the endless corrosive force of the salt, and the lack of water would take its toll. The creaking faded.

From the horizon, out where the mountains seem to float in the air, came another sound, this one more familiar to my ears. It was the methodical roar of a high-powered engine. Not an ordinary engine, but one with tremendous horsepower. Bonneville is one of the few places on the face of the Earth where you can see the curvature of the Earth, and as I stared at this phenomenon a vehicle appeared with blazing speed from the center of the curving horizon. Its speed was unbelievable, and the vehicle appeared to dance as heat waves distorted its movement. Behind it a larger rooster tail of powdered salt rose into the sky. Shaped like an oversized bullet, the vehicle had a small canopy near the point and four low-profile tires and wheels that were completely covered with body panels.

The quest for the land speed record began as early as 1911 when the 200 or so square miles of salt that are used for record runs was discovered to be useful in an unlimited release for speed. The record at that time? An incredible 50 miles per hour. Since that time man has assaulted the Flats with machines capable of awesome power. Men like Sir Malcolm Campbell and his incredible *Bluebird*, a monster that covered the measured mile required for a world record in the earth-shattering time of 301 miles per hour. The year was 1935. Captain G.E.T. Eyston upped that figure to 345 miles per hour in 1937, and if you can remember back that far you will realize that the automobile was still in its infancy. Speeds of this kind illustrate that these men had courage and ingenuity far beyond their time in history.

John Cobb came close to the 400-miles-per-hour mark in 1947 with a speed of 394.2 miles per hour and it was that magic 400-miles-per-hour number that pushed

Previous page: At the 1951 Bonneville Speed Trials, Thompson (left) raced his flathead-powered '36 Ford coupe to a speed of 141.065 miles per hour. He won the Most Determined Effort award by exhibiting the same fervor and enthusiasm that followed him throughout his life. Pioneer hot rodder and drag racer Dawson Hadley is at right.

Opposite page: In 1952, Thompson returned to the salt with a long yellow Austin Bantam coupe powered by two flatheads totaling 592 cubic inches. By the end of the meet he had reached 196.72 miles per hour, making his homemade creation the fastest coupe in the world.

In 1953 Thompson was back with the same coupe, but one of the flatheads had been replaced with perhaps the world's first blown Chrysler. It began as a $40 junk engine and a $10 4-71 blower, but it was the grandfather of the nitro-burning Hemi power plants that dominate drag racing to this day.

Mickey Thompson into his place in the history books of the Salt Flats. From the time he was seven years old, Mickey wanted to be the fastest man on wheels.

Until the early '60s, piston-driven engines were the only type used for land speed record runs, and to Mickey Thompson, the piston engine record was the only one that counted. Some men, however, were interested in the ultimate speed record regardless of the type of propellant used. In 1963, Craig Breedlove astounded the world with a run of 407 miles per hour in his *Spirit of America* jet-powered stream-liner. A fellow named Art Arfons followed several years later with a blast of 434 miles per hour in a vehicle aptly named the *Green Monster*. Breedlove came back with a new car and moved the record into the 500-miles-per-hour range (555.127, to be exact). Then the unearthly speed of 600.601 miles per hour was reached by Breedlove in an all-new vehicle called *Spirit of America Sonic I*. In 1970, a close personal friend of mine named Gary Gabelich climbed into a bullet-shaped, three-wheel, rocket-powered vehicle called *The Blue Flame* and set an all-time record of 622.40 miles per hour.

Not everyone who has run the salt has been a record setter. For some it has been the same story repeated over and over: frustration, failure, and heartbreak. For some the search for speed was too much of a strain either on their machines or themselves and death put an end to their quest.

Mickey's triumph, as you will see, was nothing short of an impossible task. Only his courage and determination allowed him to drive a piston-powered vehicle over 400 miles per hour. The speed, although historic, is really irrelevant to the struggle within this man to gain the record because, as has been the case so many times during his life, fate pulled the glory of the record from his grasp only seconds after he had perpetuated it.

In order to set a land speed record at Bonneville an average must be taken of two runs, one in the opposite direction of the other. After running 406 miles per hour, Mickey was unable to back up the record with a return run due to mechanical problems. His one-way time stands as the fastest for a piston-driven vehicle, but his name remains unlisted as the official record holder. Still, his battle with the salt is the one period of time upon which his public life has been built. And it was this fame that became the foundation of his wealth, making him a millionaire before he was thirty.

As we began to tape, I knew that the land speed record meant a great deal to Mickey; I could see it in his eyes. He enjoyed living and reliving every moment and he was proud of his accomplishments. His ego also enjoyed reminiscing.

I sat and watched dull eyes light up as Mickey began to speak of his beloved Salt Flats. "As my mother told you earlier, the first time I saw the Salt Flats was in 1937. I knew right then and there that I wanted to be the fastest man in the world behind the wheel of an automobile." He stopped for a moment, and then spoke directly to me. "You think that the story about me wanting to race for the land speed record since I was a kid is a lot of crap, don't you?" The question threw me off guard and I stammered for an answer. I agreed that I thought it was a little hard to believe that a child of eight or nine years of age could be so decisive about his life. Mickey reiterated, "Well, believe it or not, that's the truth. There was a man whom I deeply admired and tried to emulate, kind of like hero worship you might say. He was uneducated in formal schooling, but he was a genius when it came to the automobile.

"His name was Frank Lockhart and he drove at Indy. He was one of the first men to try and break the land speed record on the sand beaches at Daytona, Florida, but he was killed there around 1928 I think. Anyway, he raced by living

Besides managing a drag strip, running a muffler shop, and building race cars, Thompson's full-time occupation was as a pressman for the *Los Angeles Times*. Thompson shows a press plate to *Times* Publisher Otis Chandler as a co-worker looks on.

from hand to mouth on many occasions. Even at the time of his death he had received only enough money from a sponsor to cover the expense of building the car and he was forced to make his record attempts on inferior tires. The result was a blowout when he was going somewhere in the neighborhood of 190 miles per hour. Despite the fact that he was dead, I still read every scrap of information I could get my hands on and I knew then that something was driving me. I wasn't just an ordinary kid." Mickey stopped, and then began again in defense of his statement. "You know, I'm not trying to sound conceited when I say that I was different. I just couldn't help the feelings that were driving me. I could care less about most of the things that interested children my own age. All I cared about were cars and things that were mechanical." With this, Mickey drew his mind into a long pause before continuing.

"I missed the first year of what has now become the official Speed Week. Up until the late '40s there weren't any real organizations that held regular meets at the salt. Finally, the Southern California Timing Association began what has come to be known as the Bonneville National Speed Trials, and they are held in late August or early September, depending on the condition of the salt. Anyway, I missed the first meeting because I simply didn't have any money. I had a car, an old '36 Ford coupe, but times were tough, the war had just ended, and jobs were hard to get. Just like today, money was tough to come by.

"The following year, however, I hustled enough to buy fuel for the car and pay for food. I put the gas on a credit card and figured I would find a way to pay for it later." With that, Mickey smiled, raised his eyebrows, and commented, "Things don't change much over the years, do they?

"When I finally got to the salt, I was extremely eager—man, I wanted to set some records—but it was still the same old story, I was always a buck short. At the

Thompson and then-wife Judy work on their twin-Chrysler dragster in their El Monte, California, driveway.

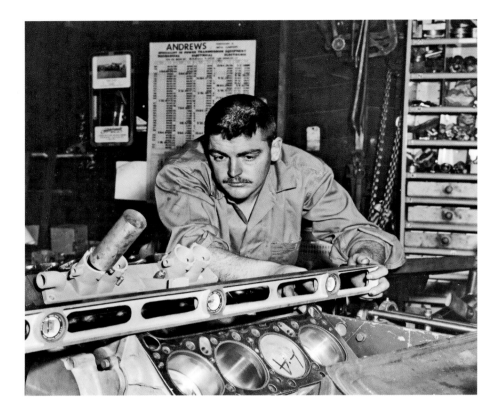

Thompson is seen working on his four-engine *Challenger* streamliner that began as a chalk outline on the home garage floor.

dry lakes, I could make the engine live because the entire run was only a mile or so, but at Bonneville there was a [long way] before the mile that was timed. I was forced to run all stock running gear and when I would get the car really running, the fuel, being much more powerful than pump gasoline, would burn a hole in one of the pistons. It was just a matter of chemistry. For example, I would run five miles over the record one way, then on the way back about halfway through the course the engine would just quit running. I guess I had too much incentive and not enough sense to quit. I would get so mad that I would try and will the engine to keep going. Many a time I came close to breaking a knuckle or two punching the dash to vent my anger. I wanted to win so bad that my mind would not accept defeat. The more problems that developed, the more of a state of frenzy I would be in."

As Mickey continued, I began to sense a quickening in my feelings toward my faith in this story. At first a battle had raged within me to create a literary masterpiece rather than just trying to capture some insight into Mickey's character. I was writing the story, but it was work; I had to force myself. One evening, while Mickey and I were taping this chapter I expressed my problem to him. He informed me that he had been aware of my problem for some time and couldn't figure out why anyone would do something that he didn't completely enjoy to the absolute limit of his consciousness. In fact, he put it rather bluntly, as he always did when he had something that needed to be said. He accused me of being either lazy or having to force myself to work. I agreed to the latter.

As we continued to talk, I began to relax. I assumed it was my association with Mickey that caused the change. But regardless of its derivation, I stopped trying so hard to write a masterpiece and decided to reach my goal the same way as my subject: in the straightest, most yielding path possible. As Mickey related his Bonneville experiences, I began to understand how and why his life path was charted as it was.

Mickey began again. "I had no choice but to haul my broken machine back home and try and figure out a way to beat the salt. I was getting all of my parts from in back of the local Ford dealer's garage, so this will give you some idea of the quality of the equipment I was using. To combat blowing the engine, I figured out that the connecting rods would have to be stronger. As a last resort, I began cutting old rods in two and piecing the discarded rods together. To ensure that they stayed together, I welded a bolt onto either side of the rod shank. Little did I know that these butchered, makeshift components would be the forerunners of the boxed rod. All I knew was that they held together for a full run at the salt. And I had to conquer that salt!"

As Mickey recounted his story, the same pattern began to form that had expressed itself in every effort he undertook. He had to scrimp and save and make do with what he had. For the next hour of taping Mickey talked of his methods. Like a pack rat, he nibbled at discarded parts at the back doors of new car agencies, picked through the trash piles of garages, and what he couldn't find, borrow, or negotiate for, he built from the resources of his mind. He had been racing on the dry lakes of Southern California for quite some time and had developed a straightaway driving skill that made him as good as any driver at the salt. Pure guts and driving ability were never a problem. It was just the age-old combination of no money means no first-class equipment. As always, the harder things got, the more determined Mickey became. What may have started out as just a dream was now an obstacle that had to be conquered. By the act of failing, ever so slightly, his inner drive drenched his mind with the sweat of failure and from that point forward Bonneville had to be overcome. As Mickey continued the tale of his early trials at the merciless salt, I could see the determination in his eyes. He was actually reliving the experiences rather than just telling the story.

"It was obvious to me that in order to make a name for myself that I would have to stop playing games and build a car that—even if it didn't set records—would still be talked about in the press. To get sponsors, people had to hear of you. My only problem was money. I just didn't have the money to build anything. All I could do was work with what I had. Anyway, a young Mexican American named Roger Flores and I designed and built a closed-bodied coupe with two old Ford engines mounted in a straight line. We made our own couplers to hold the engines together, but looking back now I don't see how that car ran. When we arrived at the salt everyone started laughing at us. I'm telling you, Tom," Mickey gestured with his fist as he always did when he wanted to bring home a point, "those guys really ticked me off. They couldn't even find a class to put the car in, so they stuck us in a coupe class, figuring that the car was a coupe, and so that class should have the pleasure of a few laughs. I can't remember the exact record of that class, it doesn't really matter now anyway, but what does matter is the fact that on the very first run I made I bumped the record by about 30 miles per hour. Immediately they took us out of the coupe class and put the car into a belly tanker class. [After World War II, hot-rodders bought surplus wing-tip fuel tanks from Air Force bombers, then modified them to house racing engines and drivers. Their bullet-like shape made them desirable for combating wind resistance.] I loved it! The belly tankers got more press ink anyway, and brother, that's what I wanted! Within a couple of runs I went faster than most of the belly tankers and they wanted me out of their class too. The sponsoring body for the Speed Week event was then forced to make up a special class just for my car. Before we left that week I had run that old clapped-out junk box nearly 190 miles per hour. They knew Mickey Thompson was there. I suppose that sounds like I'm shooting off my mouth, doesn't it?"

As I started to answer, Mickey didn't wait. He just engaged in more self-defense. "Those people laughed at me and I just had to show them that I was capable. They didn't show much in the way of consideration for my feelings, so when I proved to them that I could get the job done I could have cared less about their feelings. It might be a little childish, looking back, but hell, I was just a kid and winning meant everything.

"It took a lot of guts to drive a car 190 miles per hour when the roll bar was made out of water pipe and the tires were used Indianapolis car tires with the treads buffed off. We drove with Levi's and T-shirts, and just a helmet and goggles. We ran fuel too! I get scared just thinking about it."

Mickey had asked my wife, Darlene, and me to join him for dinner the evening we taped the first portion of this chapter, and as we sat down to eat Mickey

Thompson smoked off the line in his twin-Chrysler dragster in early 1958. Originally built with two flatheads and the driver in between, Mickey saw the potential in Manuel Coehlo's machine, bought it, and rebuilt it as a "slingshot."

continued flashing back to the early days of his activities at the Flats. "Oh, yeah," he retorted, "we used fiberglass on that old two-engined coupe and to my knowledge that was the first time anyone had ever done that before."

During dinner Mickey quietly informed me that he had been suffering from severe abdominal pains for the past six months and it was the source of great worry to him. I agreed that for some time I had known there was some sort of problem because, at times, he seemed to be overwrought and exceptionally nervous. During our taping sessions Mickey had begun a new project dealing with off-road racing, and I had assumed that it was from this new project that the nervousness stemmed. I also teased Mickey that most of the stomach disorders that he suffered from came from eating mustard, an overabundance of mustard, on every conceivable item on his menu. He put mustard on tacos, steak, meat loaf, and chocolate chip cookies. After an extended examination it was discovered that the stomach muscles that connect or hold the stomach in place had been torn and left untreated following a motorcycle accident over a year ago. This left Mickey with continuous heartburn, daily pain, constant gas, and offensive breath. An operation was imminent, but Mickey claimed that now that he knew what the affliction was, he could cope with the pain and his worrying would end. That, I had already learned, was his way of solving a medical problem. Find out the origin of the pain and then deal with it yourself. Mickey did however ask me if we could postpone taping the real issue for this chapter—his land speed record, the record that had eluded him. I agreed and we finished dinner, a large container of mustard as a centerpiece.

At our next meeting, Mickey continued building the story of Bonneville toward its culmination. He again stressed the point that money was short and that the parts needed for any car he built had to be manufactured from whatever was at hand. This was an inherent part of his makeup. It wasn't so much an exaggeration of the truth as it was a constant reminder that he had done everything on his own and he never would let those surrounding him forget it. Ridicule doled out by those who competed against him during his Bonneville efforts cut deep into Mickey's hidden emotions, although he would never let any traces surface. Still, failure became a fear and he built a shield of indifference around his character, flaunting his self-esteem as a protective device. All throughout my close association with Mickey he always remarked his was a classic struggle against the odds, meaning those with more money. Yet most of the time he conquered the odds. I believe that this fear of failure has always been, and will continue to be, the driving force that has pushed him to accomplish his string of outlandish feats. Bonneville was only the nucleus of his achievements.

When next we met, Mickey related one of the many firsts he had in the world of speed. Again, it was nurtured by the need to outperform all others.

Reasoning that he was going fast enough for aerodynamics to play a part, Thompson saved enough to have Bob Sorrell build a streamlined shell for the racer.

"In 1951, Chrysler Corp. developed what was called the hemispherical head engine. It was a new, far-reaching concept and I was convinced from the outset that it was going to be *the* racing engine of the future. The only problem was convincing anyone else. I also believed the engine would lend itself to supercharging, so as an experiment I decided to incorporate the new Hemi with a 6.71 GMC supercharger scavenged from a diesel truck. On top of the supercharger I placed five carburetors, hoping they would provide enough fuel for the engine. There wasn't enough money to build two of these engines, so I used the old flathead and the new Hemi with the blower in tandem, with the flathead in front. You should have heard the remarks about that little move." I watched as Mickey couldn't help but laugh. For an instant he reminded me of a child who was about to pull off some act of mischief. Obviously, he enjoyed telling this story.

He began again, still trying to hold back a snicker. "The combination sounded like it had unlimited horsepower but, as I mentioned, the Hemi engine was completely new and all of the internal parts had to be built from scratch. No one really knew what to expect. Anyhow, I blew the engine up six times on successive runs. I would just about reach 200 miles per hour and then parts would start to fly. I began to believe that the laughs and guffawing had some legitimacy.

"Time after time I would run down the long mile before the start of the timed mile and each time, just as it seemed that the two engines would finally work in

unison there would be a sudden lurch. The car would dart to one side and oil smoke would fill the driver's compartment. That year was a total fiasco. However, I did learn one important fact—the blown Chrysler on fuel was the answer. The question was how to make it run.

"I decided the following year to build a dual-engined, four-wheel-drive drag car, using two blown Chrysler engines. I would run the car at the drag races and at Bonneville. As the work on the car progressed, the same old story was told. I didn't have enough money to finish the job. I became frustrated, and my temper flared every time I turned around. I was married to my first wife [Judy] then, and she was forced to put up with a lot of abuse. It seemed that my whole life was like this exact situation: Ideas would fill my head, the answers to the problems would slowly be worked out, and then the money would disappear. In every instance a project that

Previous pages: On their way to the NHRA National Drags in Oklahoma City in 1958, Thompson and trusted mechanic Fritz Voigt stopped by the Bonneville Speed Trials.

Above: Before the week was over, the drags had been forgotten, there was a pile of shredded tires and ruined Chrysler parts, and Thompson was the fastest American ever at 294 miles per hour.

I knew would work would come to a grinding halt, forcing me to go out into the business world and beg for backing. I'll tell you, that was the hardest thing in the world for me to do. Especially then, when I was practically a nobody."

Mickey stopped in the middle of his story to further defend himself against an as-yet-unmentioned accusation. "I know that my critics have accused me of being a hustler and getting money for projects from everyone under the sun. Well, I'm here to tell you right now that it was pure anguish for me to go out and beg for money. It made me hard as a rock and forced me to adopt a cold and calculating personality when it came to business. That's the way life is, but I have always tried to give a buck's worth of effort for a buck's worth of help."

As his story continued, Mickey became more defensive, bringing into focus still another facet of the Thompson personality. His drive to be the holder of the world land speed record for piston-driven vehicles was in its incubational period and for a man whose life seemed predestined, these growing pains were tempering a human personality that would soon be faced with the absolute solitude and remoteness that surrounds a man who drives himself to a twilight zone where his fellow humans would not venture.

"I did manage to make an agreement with the Firestone Tire and Rubber Company. I told them that I wanted to build a 400-miles-per-hour machine. But when I told them that I wanted to run a vehicle with four engines, their attitude was one of reluctance. As a prelude to the four-engined car, I informed Firestone that I was ready to put together a vehicle that was capable of running 300 miles per hour with two engines: the two Chryslers in the drag car. Finally, they relented and agreed that if I could go 300 miles per hour with the two-engined car that they would build tires that would run 400 miles per hour. I really couldn't blame them for their pessimistic attitude; after all, the costs involved in research and development of a completely new tire that would be used for only one purpose were staggering. It costs about $100,000 and up to produce just one tire. I had to consider the fact that if I didn't do anything but blow engines as I had in the past, then all of that money was down the drain. They wouldn't even be able to advertise the fact.

"As the car reached completion, optimism was at a low ebb. In fact, I could only afford one of the engines. It was Fritz Voigt who saved the day."

Mickey sighed. The name Fritz Voigt meant so much, from the very best to the depths of despair for Mickey. We both remembered that on the night of our first taping session Fritz had called Mickey for the first time in many years. That was the night I discovered that Mickey Thompson was an intense, sensitive person and not a crude, indifferent personality as he was sometimes portrayed. Fritz had been Mickey's friend, savior, partner, advisor, competitor, and, finally, an enemy. Then completing the circle of human emotions, Fritz called to renew his acquaintance. But in the spring of their friendship, Fritz and Mickey formed a strong alliance.

"This was the late '50s and Fritz was an outstanding drag racer in his own right. He had been running a Hemi Chrysler in a dragster and doing very well. We made a deal. He would loan me his engine, which ran on gasoline, and I would run my engine on fuel. After Bonneville I would help him at the National Drag Championships. We also decided to run both engines injected rather than blown, as I had originally intended. When we brought the car to the salt, I felt a little uncomfortable. You know how you feel sometimes when you're really worried about something? Not scared, but terribly apprehensive. I just wasn't sure. As it worked out, the next few days were to be some of the happiest and some of the most aggravating days I ever experienced at the salt."

Contrary to the press releases and previous stories about Mickey's experiences at the Flats, he had so far dispensed with the endless hours of explanation of the mechanics of the vehicles involved. We had agreed at the start to try and keep our story directed toward an insight into his inner feelings and try and determine what it was that made him different from other men. Now as we approached the most significant time period of his life, I was elated as an author that Mickey was willing to speak honestly about his feelings and to reveal his as-yet-unrecorded thoughts. I could, however, feel the tension in his voice as he spoke about trying to run 300 miles per hour in a vehicle that was, by his own admission, not the safest projectile in the world. This tension had stayed with him for fourteen years.

"When Fritz and I were ready, we rolled out the project of our joint venture long before the sun ever showed an indication of light. It's always cold and lonely those few moments before dawn. I guess all of those sayings about the darkest hour before the dawn are true. The salt is a very noiseless place before sunrise.

"There were only a few people who would attest to the runs. Nameless faces, men who had seen bigger names than Mickey Thompson and who were only here to do a job. I couldn't really blame anyone for their sentiments; after all, they were unaware of my sensations as a child of nine, standing in this place knowing that someday I would drive a car faster than anyone else. They didn't perceive the fervor I felt as I slid into the cockpit of the car.

"Anyway, Fritz and I nodded at each other and our struggle began. Just as I was about to begin the first run, a member of the timing crew leaned over inside the car and told me to try and go over 150 miles per hour if I could. That made me furious. If I hadn't been strapped into the confines of that cockpit I would have climbed out and told that guy what he could do with his advice. As the vehicle began to pick up speed, vibration set in and the car began to hunt and dart. The noise was deafening and there was nothing to use as reference for calculating speed. I knew I was going fast, but I didn't know how fast. You know how it is?"

We paused and for a few minutes it was my turn to relive a few moments of my own at the Flats. Mickey's half-heckling remark sent my mind back to October of 1968. We began to talk about how the Ford Motor Company and Mickey had gotten together to make an attempt to capture all of the endurance records for stock cars at the Bonneville Salt Flats. A 10-mile oval track was marked off and two Ford Mustangs were specially built for the task. The course was marked with tiny red flags that were embedded in the salt's surface. It was decided to run the two Mustangs day and night, so smudge pots—squat, flat-bottomed containers filled with coal oil—were stationed adjacent to the flags. The marked-off course measured exactly 10 miles in circumference. The cars involved in the event differed only in engine size. One contained a big-block, 427-cubic-inch engine, the other was a smaller 302-cubic-inch engine similar to the engine used by Ford in several other racing ventures. This was when Ford was deeply involved in a racing program, before tight budgets and engine restrictions.

I was one of several press journalists invited to attend these record attempts. It was my first trip to the salt, and I became enthralled with the salt's immensity and the ease with which it could affect the human body. Despite the fact that the space designated at the pit area was busy with mechanics, public relations personnel, and press, the salt, with its immense size, shadowed these intruders as if they did not exist. If you moved a hundred yards from the main body of voices and sounds, their prattle became muffled by the emptiness.

I was chosen to be a passenger with Mickey for a demonstration ride around the 10-mile oval. It was a rather dubious honor to say the least. If he or I knew then that a few years later I would be recording his life story, a few concessions might have been made.

The crackling of the unmuffled engine was deafening as several crew members strapped me into the passenger's seat. Naturally, rides were given in the car with the largest engine—the strongest running of the two cars. As we left the pit area, the car quickly picked up speed. As we accelerated, Mickey, with a cat-like motion, snapped the steering wheel to the left and then to the right. This action sent the car spinning in a 360-degree circle. Shock must have covered my face, as Mickey laughed hysterically. He pounded the wheel as his broad smile met my frozen stare.

With the car running in a straight line Mickey suddenly collected his smile into a firm, set jaw. A steady thrust of power propelled us deep into the nothingness of the salt. The smell of overheated tires and a hard-working clutch filled the cockpit as the car continued to gain velocity. I could barely see the tiny flags and smudge

Above: During record attempts at Bonneville, the crew found shade under an airplane wing. Fighting weather and mechanical problems, the officials suggested that Thompson might be better off going after world records from five kilometers to ten miles. These records were easily broken with a best two-way average of 345.33 miles per hour before weather ended the '59 effort.

Right: On August 9, 1959, test runs were made at Edwards Air Force Base—formerly Muroc Dry Lake, hot rodding's birthplace. The accelerating *Challenger* hit an unseen bump, went airborne for sixty-six feet, and spun out at over 200 miles per hour. Thompson was shaken but learned a lot that day.

pots as they blurred past the window. They had been placed at 100-yard intervals, but they flashed by as if they were only inches apart. It was now time to take the first turn. Mickey again snapped the car into a long lazy slide and salt blew up under the floorboard. The engine never changed pitch; the markers flashed by at the same rate. As we slid, Mickey worked the steering wheel from side to side, keeping the car drifting. It was obvious that he was in complete control. His face was placid; he seemed to be daydreaming or maybe planning his method of driving during the twenty-four hours that lay ahead. Slowly, I began to enjoy the ride. The involvement was stimulating and made me feel totally free as we sailed across the limitless salt.

On the horizon a tiny speck materialized into our starting point and my body pushed against the seat belts as we decelerated to a halt.

For the next twenty-four hours Mickey and his co-driver, Danny Ongais, negotiated the 10-mile oval at speeds over 180 miles per hour. During the night I sat on a lawn chair outside the press trailer and stared into the bottomless pit that

Above: Thompson looked optimistic as *Challenger* came together.

Opposite page: The twin-Chrysler streamliner in the El Monte driveway had to share garage space with the Kurtis sports car

lay before me. Only the flickering of the coal oil lights could be seen in the distance. Only the roar of the engine was audible. Every few minutes a car would flash by. It seemed as if a dream were being projected before my eyes. Around midnight one of the cars broke down and Mickey, his face covered with oil smudge, busted into the trailer to announce that it was his birthday and cake and coffee would be served. Everyone sang and laughed and licked icing from their fingers. I remember Mickey laughing. Then, as if realizing this was out of character, he became concerned and pensive as a roar from outside brought reality into the emptiness that surrounded us.

Without warning, Mickey made a quick motion with his hand that brought me back to the present with a jolt. I was quickly learning to hate his manner of breaking the conversation off whenever it took a turn he did not like. He wanted to talk about the experience leading up to his record attempts as if nothing else mattered. The incident passed with nothing more than a touch of anger on my part, but I realized that there were tremendous contradictions in our personalities and the consideration shown so far for each other's feelings was growing thin.

"One of the saddest memories I have about my experiences at Bonneville concerns the friendships that exist between competitors who race only a clock. At a banquet one evening during Speed Week a man by the name of Bill Kenz complimented me on the progress that I had been making running the dual-engined coupe. He wanted to express his interest and extend any help that he might be able to give. At the time he held the record for vehicles running two engines. He explained that within a few years he felt that I would be extremely competitive. As he spoke, I felt a little rude about my thoughts. In effect, my subconscious told me that if I didn't beat his record that year that things were all over for me. I wasn't playing games: Firestone had backed me against the wall with the promise of building a set of tires that would hold up under the punishment of an all-out land speed record, if I went 300 miles per hour or over that year. Anyway, Bill was standing on the starting line before the first really hard run on that car and he wished me good luck as I left.

"As the car rolled to a stop, five miles from the point of origin, I knew I had gone fast, but as I mentioned, you just have no way of estimating speed. As I sat waiting for the pickup crew to come down and get me, my thoughts returned to Bill Kenz. What if I had beaten his record? It had taken him three years to set a new speed for the class and here I was, a comparative newcomer, in a backyard monster, with one engine running on gas and the other running on fuel. I was very afraid that my run might make him look foolish. As it turned out, I had run some 20 miles per hour faster than any run ever made in the dual-engined class. A shade under 272 miles per hour. The instant I heard the news, I forgot about anyone else's feelings. I knew then that I would be able to run 300 miles per hour, get the bigwigs at Firestone interested enough to keep their word and build tires for an all-out record run. Man, I was really happy! My feelings were short-lived, however, because from that point on events turned into the proverbial 'can of worms.'

"Whenever the car would go over the 290-miles-per-hour mark, a terrible vibration began. I couldn't keep the car on the salt. It shook so hard that holding the wheel took all the effort I could manage. At that speed it only takes an instant to move from a situation you have under control to an out-of-control situation. Once a vehicle becomes hard to handle at that speed you have to be a fool to not be frightened. And Tom, I was scared on every run.

"We traced the problem to the tires. At 290-miles-per-hour, or close to that figure, the tires would throw the rubber off the tread. When I complained to Firestone about the breakdown of the tires, they informed me that it was the tire growing from centrifugal force, hitting the aluminum body of the car, that was tearing the rubber off. I contended that it was the fact that the tires just couldn't absorb the punishment of a 300-miles-per-hour run. They stood firm, and so did I."

Once again, Mickey pointed an accusing finger in my face to illustrate his insistence. "Tom," he continued, "I knew the car had the power to go 300 miles per hour and I was just as convinced that my theory was accurate about the tires. To prove my point, on the last run, I grabbed a hand ax in a fit of anger and chopped holes in the body panels. In the beautiful, hand-pounded aluminum body that just a few weeks ago I had sweated and slaved over to perfect the design. Now I had ripped giant, ugly holes into it. But at least the tires, when they expanded, would have nothing to buff against.

"When I began the run, I sat in the cockpit and watched the tires through the holes. At 290 miles per hour I actually saw the rubber peel off and scatter like an explosion. I became so furious that I just stayed on the gas. I wanted to go to 300 miles per hour. Firestone had promised me help if I could do it. The vibration began but I stayed on the gas. Things got worse; the canopy blew off and a near 300-miles-per-hour gust of wind tore into my face, forcing my head against the roll bar. Parts began to fly, and the car literally began to shake itself to pieces. The run was timed at 298 miles per hour, very close to the mark I needed.

"After it was over, and there was no chance to rebuild for another assault, I went to Firestone to see if I could persuade them to go ahead with plans to build a 400-miles per hour tire. The representative said something to the effect of 'no 300-miles-per-hour mark, no tires.' The frustration was almost overwhelming. I later concluded that they couldn't build the tire, or at least they were not sure they could, and therefore took refuge in the agreement we had made."

For the 1960 record attempts, the nose and tail were reworked extensively. With the addition of four superchargers, the hood was redesigned with big air scoops.

It was obvious that the agreement cut deeply into Mickey's goals because, as we taped, he continually referred to the fact that Firestone had made a promise and then used the two- or three-miles-per-hour difference as a scapegoat to get out of building a 400-miles-per-hour tire. He also commented that the representative with whom he had arranged the original agreement was dismissed after the controversy.

I had decided to dispense with the actual details of how the *Challenger I* had been assembled. The hours of sweat, trial and error, tears, experimenting, frustration, aggravation, and eons of labor have already been recorded and re-recorded time after time. I wanted to study the man under the most adverse conditions. He was aiming for a feat never before accomplished. No man had ever strapped himself into a machine powered by four 1,000-horsepower engines

Posing for its 1959 portrait, *Challenger* is amazingly small considering the amount of horsepower it contains. Beside it, the previous British land speed machines would look like locomotives.

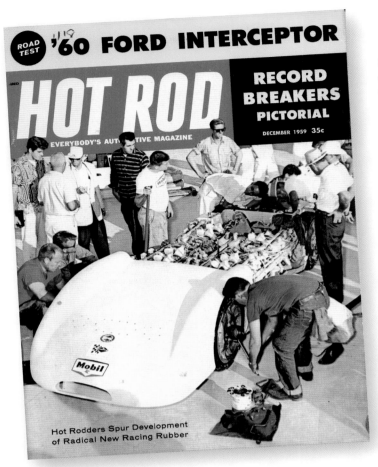

Above: The cover of the December 1959 issue of *Hot Rod* magazine showed Thompson (holding jack handle) and crew at Edwards Air Force Base. The caption called it "The man, the car, and the crew most likely to succeed as the World's Fastest."

Following pages: The late afternoon sun forms long shadows on the salt as starter Bob Higbee (above front wheel) signals Thompson and crew to begin another run.

to propel himself across a barren stretch of wasteland at a speed of over 400 miles per hour. Yet this is what Mickey faced. His method of solving these apparently insurmountable problems was what interested me most.

Before we met for the final taping session, the gap that had opened ever so slightly a few weeks prior continued to widen. Mickey was in the process of finalizing his new idea in off-road racing. He was building an entire organization called SCORE (Short Course Off-Road Events), something that had never been done before. And it seemed as if these pressures, coupled with reliving the frustration he experienced at Bonneville, brought forth a new aspect of his personality. He constantly displayed a sense of pressure and urgency about every moment of the day. For several days running he would make inferences during our telephone conversations that "the impossible only takes a little longer."

When I admitted that the writing was progressing poorly, he turned cold, and his eyes took on a new dimension in chilliness. He was working twenty hours a day on his project, and he saw no reason why everyone around him should not follow suit. Fatigue racked his body. His eyes were sunken and his usual act of playing tired for sympathy was now a reality. During the infrequent times he would spare a moment to speak to me, he was forced to lie on a couch in his office and rest while we talked. Very little was accomplished.

In the seclusion of my private office the conflict grew worse. The pressure of doing a good job and getting it done quickly forced me into a self-inflicted mental block. The words stayed imprisoned in my mind. Any reason was good enough to avoid working. I became irritated and overly sensitive. Sleep became difficult. As the frustration built, my surroundings lost their comforting effects, and home and family—especially my wonderful wife—were targets for my hypersensitivity. Out of utter desperation I stayed up all one night to see if the weariness that came over me would soothe my anxieties. Nothing worked and the pages stayed in my typewriter for longer and longer periods before completion.

Above: In the late afternoon, *Challenger*'s blue paint seemed to blend with the sky and long shadows. Thompson is at right in motorcycle leathers holding his helmet.

A sense of guilt was next. I was writing only words; why would such a simple act as writing words become so difficult? Rest was impossible. I remained haunted by the thought that the man putting the pressure on me was the same man whom I had approached and convinced that I was the one person who had the ability to record the events that had made him what he was. And now, I was unable to carry on because I could not compete with my subject. He had the capabilities to drive himself day and night to accomplish his goals. Now as we approached the reliving of his greatest moment, he seemed to drive himself even harder. After all, by his own admission, he had worked three jobs in order to build the land speed record car; he worked at the *Los Angeles Times* newspaper, in a garage in which he was a part owner, and on the project he called *Challenger I.* There are only twenty-four hours in a day, yet here was a man who could apparently function for that amount of time without the luxury of rest.

As we prepared to record the final segments of the events of the record run, both Mickey and I were in a state of mental tension. The date of his off-road event was near, and he was extremely edgy. I was trying to find a relief in the pressure brought on by Mickey's demanding manner; his reliving the occurrences leading to the record attempts seemed to both invigorate and depress him.

The car, called *Challenger I,* was built, for all practical purposes, in Mickey's backyard with the help of a young Mexican American named Rodger Flores. They received help on the aerodynamic design from George Hill, also a Bonneville racer. The aluminum body was constructed by Don Borth. Mickey wanted to use Chrysler Hemi engines but ended up using Pontiac engines. The Pontiacs were lighter,

Goodyear organized the grand unveiling of *Challenger* at the Beverly Hilton Hotel before its first trip to Bonneville in 1959.

produced a good rate of horsepower per cubic inch, and were free. ("My lifelong friend Bunkie Knudsen came to my aid," Mickey explained.) Mobil Oil, a company involved with many land speed record attempts, offered their financial support and the Goodyear Tire and Rubber Company, with Mickey's suggestions, designed and built a 400-miles-per-hour tire. Still, with all the help he received, Mickey basically built the car from the ground up without the benefit of blueprints or engineering help from outside sources. Despite his wide and varied background in automobile race car building, the fact that he was able to build a four-engined vehicle capable of running in a straight line at better than 400 miles per hour is incredible.

Observing Mickey the week before I taped the final interview portion regarding his record run, I could understand how the feat of building the *Challenger I* was accomplished by this truly unusual man. At Riverside Raceway, the site of a most important off-road race for SCORE, he turned from a man into a frenzied spirit. Dressed in old tattered jeans with a two-way radio stuffed conspicuously in his waistband, Mickey sweated, cursed, playacted, conned, jousted, barked orders, and drove around the course like a man possessed. He savagely tore at misplaced hay bales and more or less directed the entire operation as he charmed the press and competitors alike. Even those who openly criticized the effort were humbled into submission.

Mickey rested on a sofa and stared at the ceiling as he began talking about a lifetime of dreams. He spoke softly as he recounted his feelings about the huge deficit between his attempts and those of other notables who had tried and failed to surpass the 400-miles-per-hour mark. He was shown little in the manner of respect by the officials at the Salt Flats. There were few who really believed that this upstart hot-rodder with the brash, pushy personal habits would inflict much of a dent in the existing records—let alone set any goals of his own.

After a deliberate pause, Mickey talked of his deep feelings for Fritz, the man who stood by his every effort and provided the manual labor necessary to complete each and every job as it appeared. Without Fritz, there would have been no record. Tears filled his eyes as he spoke of his first wife, Judy, and how her emotions were strained to the limit. Within several years this tremendous pressure would tear them apart and shatter their lives. He had consummated his lifelong goal of becoming the fastest man on earth, but for those who aided him the price was high.

For hours Mickey talked about wet salt, mechanical failures, terrifying spins at 300 miles per hour, despair, heartbreak, fires, arguments, design errors, tires that had blown to pieces, sleepless nights, and confusion, but no record. Finally, the salt went bad and 1959 ended in failure. Another failure that tore the soul of a man who hated to be second.

In 1960 Mickey Thompson came back to the salt, better prepared than the previous year, yet still hopelessly outclassed by his competitors as far as finances were concerned. The *Challenger I* had been rebuilt; superchargers were added to the engines, developing double the horsepower compared to the previous year. Having seen the *Challenger* firsthand many years ago, I can attest to the fact that the vehicle was sensuous in its beauty. The smooth, graceful lines were soothing yet savage when you considered controlling its devastating potential. Its personality reflected only a semblance of the brusqueness of its builder.

Again in 1960, the unyielding salt forced bone-jarring control problems, out-of-control situations, terror-filled moments, engine explosions, transmission failures, and despair. Tire balance problems were traced, and the speed climbed to 375 miles per hour. The tire failure was traced to out-of-round tires. A matched set was tested on a machine that spun the tires to nearly 500 miles per hour to check their ability to stay round. The tire problem was solved.

Mickey was zealous as he began to speak. "You know, Tom, the one feeling that I have never been able to get across to anyone was the feeling of utter loneliness that I got that morning as I slid into the *Challenger I*. To go over 300 miles per hour in a land vehicle is a tremendous strain. It drains you from your tiniest muscle deep into your mind. By the time we found what all the problems were, I was so desperate that no one could stand being around me. On that final morning as I buckled my seat belts and pulled

Thompson seems to be wondering how he'll find enough room for four fuel tanks in the nose of his relatively small streamliner.

the oxygen mask over my face, I felt that my energies had reached their pinnacle. I wasn't sure how much longer I could go on.

"Then, somewhere about midrange on the course I got a feeling, a tingle down inside. The engines pounded in my ears, the car's acceleration pulled hard at my guts. Man, I was running hard and I knew it." Mickey pounded the coffee table with his fist as he continued. "The car darted, but I kept control. I was going faster than anyone had ever gone before. I was doing something man would do for the first time—go over 400 miles per hour in a race car. I was doing it! Me, Mickey Thompson! Nobody could laugh—I showed everyone that I knew what the hell I was talking about—I did it!

Of the nearly countless race cars owned and driven by Mickey Thompson, *Challenger* and *Assault* (both pictured above) are known to be his two favorites.

"As the car rolled to a stop, I didn't need a timing slip. I knew that I had gone over 400—406 miles per hour, to be exact. All I needed was a record on the return run and my name would go down in the book of speed with all those brave men before me. I was so excited—I was one of them—the men I had admired all of my life."

Suddenly the smile that had enveloped Mickey's face disappeared as he spoke of the return run for the record. "You know about the return run: A driveshaft broke and that ended that." As he concluded his last remark he changed the subject. "There is nothing more I can say. I went back to the salt with another car sponsored by Ford, but it never came close to breaking the record. Then I broke my back and never tried for the land speed record again. Now, of course, the record is over 600 miles per hour and I'll never get another chance."

In 1969, Thompson holds a press conference on the salt as he and Danny Ongais prepare to set hundreds of endurance records in three specially prepared Ford Mustangs.

There are some postscripts to this story. Mickey's name did not go down in the record books because of the lack of a backup run, and since that day records have become a stigma to his personality. After Bonneville, he built numerous cars and systemically set record after record, at drag strips, old Air Force bases, even Bonneville, but he never again broke the land speed record. He built his fantastic reputation on a single 406-mile-per-hour run. He became the world's fastest man in one direction. But he still carries the scar of that failed backup run.

There is an empty lot adjacent to Mickey's shop in Long Beach, California. It is filled with remnants of old discarded race cars. There are successes and there are failures. Twisted and broken they lay, even a burned-out hulk in which a man died. All rust in a limbo of indifference. Under the pile of discards rests a beaut of a car, four-engined and smooth of body. It has been discarded by its owner, as a cruel person would discard a friend who is no longer of any use. As I stared at the hulk I became melancholy and wondered whether I wasn't making a mistake by continuing this project.

Trophies from the 1959 and 1960 Bonneville Speed Trials seem to arouse a sea of memories in Thompson's mind.

CHAPTER

6

THE BEST
OF TIMES
THE WORST
OF TIMES

For the second time—and possibly the last time—since this book's inception I have solicited a source other than Mickey Thompson as a quarry for information. His mother had provided the hypothesis for his early attributes. She gave me insight into his childhood. The combination of these basic facts brought into focus the development of Mickey's personality. However, there now arose a deficiency for the same evaluation as an adult. A fail-safe to ensure the validity of Mickey's own statements was also needed. He had shown an active ego, a condition that sometimes uses exaggeration to satisfy a hunger. I needed a view from an opposing direction. A man from his past by the name of Fritz Voigt was my selection as the person to fill that void.

Fritz had acted as Mickey's accomplice throughout his greatest triumphs and his most ridiculed follies. Constantly placed in the background, Fritz Voigt performed as *se tirer d'affaire* at Bonneville, at Indy, at drag races, and a host of record-setting attempts by Mickey whenever he became possessed by the devil speed. He had lived, slept, sweated, drank, cursed, become fatigued, and agonized with and because of Mickey Thompson for more than ten years. They had used each other. They had become friends, then adversaries, and friends once again. Fritz Voigt knew my subject as well as any person could and seemed a logical choice. And as the story began to unfold no choice could have been better.

Fritz was born of German ancestry fifty years prior to our meeting. He is a thick, muscular man. His face is long, and his features are etched in sharp, precise lines. Thinning black hair is combed straight back. His hands, creased with black lines from years of toiling in the grease, show their age. His eyes are set deep and forever analyzing what they view. His voice shows a slight trace of an accent. Fritz is crude most times in his mannerisms. And, by his own admission, he was the person singled out by God to invent profanity.

Fritz had not spoken to Mickey, except through an intermediary, for several years. Then, as if prearranged, Fritz called one evening while Mickey and I struggled through one of the earlier tapes. Thus, from out of the past, Fritz was interjected into a story that could not have been complete without his presence.

Previous page: Judy Thompson gives Mickey a congratulatory kiss after he set four world records. Fritz Voigt looks on.

Within a month, arrangements were made for Fritz and I to meet and tape his feelings of his relationship with Mickey and his conclusions concerning why or what made Thompson what he is.

On the morning I left for our first meeting many preconceived thoughts swirled in my mind. Fritz was not on the best of terms with Mickey, despite the fact that they had resumed speaking person to person. He had agreed to tell the truth, but telephone conversations led to the inference that with the truth would run rivers of bitterness. Fritz was personally very close to Mickey's ex-wife, Judy—a subject that so far had been a forbidden topic.

Reportedly, Fritz had been moderately successful in business. But after several telephone conversations, I had the feeling that his place of business was less than expansive. He worked by appointment only; lately, by his own admission, he had little motivation or appointments.

Twenty minutes of strenuous address hunting passed before I located Fritz's shop. Unmarked, it was situated in a commercial area of the city, wedged between two large industrial complexes, neither of which served any automotive needs. There were no markings or advertising signs, nothing to resurrect the Voigt Garage from its obvious place of hiding.

Bound on either side by walls and fortified in front by a sliding chain-link gate, in reality, Voigt's Garage was an expanse of concrete covered by the shadows of two large buildings, for all practical purposes forgotten by time. Scattered, stacked, and discarded here were literally thousands of whole and dismembered auto parts. Gear grease was the most predominant aroma. Remnants of the past were everywhere. The term "junkyard" is too cruel. Junkyards are cold and ruthless; memories cannot live where every decision is of dollars and cents. There was nothing repugnant here. All was safe; no memories would be sold for money.

In the rear of the shop rested an office, or at least what could pass as a facsimile. It too was filled to capacity with inventory. Posters advertising drag race events that had long since been laid to rest occupied strategic locations on the walls. They hung stained from inactivity as old skid row drunks cling to the walls of a welfare mission.

In the midst of his kingdom stood Fritz. His greeting was warm. He apologized, then cursed for the condition of things such as they were.

After several minutes of exchanging pleasantries, during which Fritz seemed uncomfortable, the mood for our meeting shifted somewhat. There was no room among the remnants for us to work adequately. Fritz cursed, "Well, goddammit, I'm not use to having somebody poking around here."

He next brushed off a customer, who had wandered in from the street through the unattended gate, which had been left unguarded after my entering.

Thompson is making sure "Jazzy" Nelson is using only pump gas to power his record-breaking entry.

Fritz simply told the man, without much study, that whatever it was he was after, it wasn't available.

Because of our cramped quarters, our taping session was forced into the confines of my pickup truck, with the tape recorder perched atop the truck's hood, a microphone cable running from outside, through a window into the cab. Next, an extension cord had to be manufactured from scraps of wiring in order to gain power from an isolated electrical outlet. Fritz hadn't given many interviews over the years.

With an inelegant gesture, Fritz then dismissed a young helper who had been off in the shadows until this point. He then dropped the wall-mounted telephone from its hanger, rendering it useless, picked up the tape recorder's microphone, and began.

"Naturally I met Mickey at the drag races. That's where this whole business began. I guess I was involved before Mickey; I had heard of him, but didn't think very much about it. Every time I saw him, he reminded me of an ignorant, egotistical sort, and I never went out of my way to meet anyone like that."

A broad smile splashed across Fritz's face as he slowly brushed back the years and began to concentrate on our project.

"You know, Mickey always ran with the high-dollar boys, the ones with the money. At the time I had a flaky garage and a flaky race car. The only reason I raced was for the sheer pleasure involved. Not Mickey. Man, that guy raced for blood! Even if I would have wanted to talk to him, once a race was underway all he would do was thrash on his car.

"Finally, it was my ex-wife and Mickey's ex-wife Judy who sort of arranged our meeting. Both Mickey and I ran at Long Beach Drag Strip every weekend. And both of us ran for Top Eliminator. Usually, this was the last race of the evening. After the racing was over, it was late. Those of us that were left would hang around and BS, or bench race would be a better word. Eventually we became friends.

"Somewhere along the line, don't ask me exactly where 'cause I can't remember, Mickey bought an old dual-engined dragster to rebuild for the Bonneville Salt Flats. It was a real hulk. I was just about ready to quit driving. Drag racing had become boring as hell. And my garage was full of crap that I was getting ready to pitch. Mickey needed an engine and most of the equipment to go with it. In my shop, piled in various stages of deterioration, were Chrysler Hemi engine parts, the very parts that Mickey was searching for. Everybody at that time was using Hemi engines. Mickey, being the smooth-talking hustler that he is, convinced me to throw in with him. We built a front-mounted, dual-engined race car."

Fritz laughed uproariously. "You know we broke a lot of records in that old crap-box."

Instinctively, Fritz raised a corpulent hand to his mouth in mock mortification.

"Mickey is goin' to raise hell about my language when he reads this. In fact, he'll probably throw the whole damn chapter about me in the trash can. You know, he doesn't want anyone to think he swears. It's bad for his image. Well, I'm here to tell you that sometimes he overdoes that image crap. When we were racing, Mickey cursed plenty. Now he wants everyone to think he has changed his ways. Hell, swearing doesn't mean a man is good or bad inside. Does it?"

Fritz ran his hand through his thinning hair and directed the remainder of his commentary on the art of cursing toward himself.

"I'm kind of an ignorant, crude bastard and I've been around race cars, grease, and this flaky garage so long that swearing is the only way I can communicate.

When I call some guy a son of a bitch, that means I like him and acknowledge him as a human. I think something of him. I don't really mean the words. On the other hand, if I refer to a guy by his name, that means I have no interest in him at all."

Fritz shrugged and nudged my shoulder with the tips of his fingers in a slapping motion and quipped, "That's enough bullshit about me, let's talk about Mickey or his ego will start getting jealous and put a curse on us.

"It was coming home from Bonneville in late summer of '58, after we had run really fast with the dual-engined car, that Mickey and I became a team. We had run 290 miles per hour, or some such number, and Mickey was sitting in the back seat of an old Caddy I owned. We were driving down from Salt Lake. Anyhow, Mickey says, 'You know, Fritz, goddammit, I'm going to get the land speed record!' I laughed, 'Mickey you're full of crap.' But it didn't matter, he just kept talking. He said, 'No, I got it all figured out.'

"Obviously, he had been thinking about this for a long time. Looking back now after all these years, I believe that old story his father used to tell about Mickey standing on the salt when he was a tyke and saying that he would hold the record as the fastest man on earth.

"No one tried to stop him, although we all thought he was crazy. He went to Chrysler to get engines for the project and they laughed at him, thinking the project a farce. Well, rejection just turns Mickey on. He cornered a friend of his at Pontiac who became interested in racing and Pontiac then fronted for about six or eight engines. Then the battle began.

"There is only one point I want to make, because I realize that his record attempts have already been discussed. However, I want people to fully understand that no one had ever undertaken a project of this type, running a vehicle using four internal combustion engines, prior to Mickey's attempt at the land speed record. What Mickey did was all his, and it was strictly an American effort to bring the land speed record back to America. That's what's so damn significant about it!

"I knew how determined he could get when he wanted something, so after listening to this theories Mickey convinced me it would work. We agreed that Mickey would build the chassis and design everything pertaining to the aerodynamics. I would build the engines and running gear (driveshafts, rear ends, transmissions, etc.).

"In a way, I was kind of glad Mickey had conceded that I should build the engines. He's a good enough backyard mechanic, but I would never let him build a racing engine for me that I had to depend on. He gets too damn nervous when he works. Mickey has a habit of starting a thousand projects at one time and he gets to thinking about every deal he has going, especially promoting himself, and he forgets what the hell he's doing."

As Fritz spoke, I interrupted with a question that seemed apropos, one that pointed toward my own justification of this entire project. The answer would add another strand to the complex web woven by Thompson's personality. Why were all of Mickey's projects completed in a state of ambiguity and perplexity?

"Do you mean, why does everything Mickey has had anything to do with always end up in a half-assed condition?" Fritz answered.

He didn't wait for my reaction.

"Mickey really doesn't want to be that way, and for the most part, projects he controls just give this illusion. That's just his way. He gets too excited.

"Mickey rarely begins an undertaking without first basing everything on a sound idea. Something that he has completely thought out and knows will work. Then he surrounds himself with a competent crew. He has always had the knack for finding good help—men that will stay with him and work day and night until the job is finished. It just happens, as the tempo and pressure of one of Mickey's ideas grows, he becomes so involved that if you really don't know him you would swear that he was losing his mind. He rants and raves. He screams at the crews. Throws fits of temper; but that's just one way of building to a climax. The 'shrinks' have a name for it; I call it getting the job done. If Mickey wasn't the way he is, he would still be slinging papers for the *L.A. Times*.

"Looking back, I would venture to say that whenever one of our efforts got to the point of truly being fully organized, someone aside from Mickey was controlling events. Mickey is fundamentally a dreamer of ideas, an organizer of men, and a doer of impossible tasks. Not a nitpicker. Whenever we became involved in various business ventures together throughout the years, I would tease Mickey by telling him to handle the million-dollar deals and I would handle the five-and-dime sales."

Fritz rambled indiscriminately for the next hour or so about his relationship with Thompson. Most of those ventures (Bonneville and Indy) are discussed at length by Thompson himself within this story. This period in Fritz's life was such a powerful influence that as he spoke, he admitted he still used the first-person plural pronoun *we* when speaking of Thompson. I began to diagnose his feelings. Fritz was an open window, displaying, for a random bypasser, what an association with a temperament such as Thompson's could do to an unsuspecting soul. Here sat a man, beginning the autumn of his life, reliving a lifetime with some of its greatest moments overshadowed by the influence of a more aggressive personality.

Numerous times during our taping session, Fritz had referred to himself as a flaky, uneducated, doltish chump. He made a point to mention the fact that he had served jail terms for various shady deals. Again, downgrading himself. His vulgar, often abusive language seemed just another method of hiding his true feelings.

Admittedly, Fritz lived in somewhat of a state of confusion. He has been married four times, twice to the same woman. Jokingly he referred to time spent with his psychiatrist—"shrinks" was what he enjoyed calling his analyst—as "finding out those dumb sons of bitches had as many problems as I had, the only difference was they got paid for listening to someone who had troubles." Another of his favorite remarks was, "You can tell how screwed up I am because I had a vasectomy, then had everything reconnected, then disconnected again."

However, under this self-induced smokescreen of masochistic commentary, I discovered a man capable of warm and sometimes tender feelings. A man obviously capable of foraging for himself. A man of substantial funds needing help from no one. Fritz was basically none of the images he described, but he reveled in acts that depicted him in a degrading manner.

As he continued his story, one fact was evident. Fritz had spent his most valuable years sharing the glory of a phenomenal personality, always from the shadows. And now the shadows remained.

I continued a stringent line of interrogation by pinpointing the question of Mickey's ability as a competent race car driver as compared to other professional drivers with a similar amount of talent. Fritz's answer was typical: short and to the point.

"Well, I don't really know if you could classify his ability as being any better than other professional race drivers, but there is one fact for certain. There is no son of a bitch alive, bar none, who is braver than Mickey Thompson. I'm not sure if it's a case of 'balls' or ego; it doesn't really matter. For the most part, in MT's life anyway, the two—bravery and ego—are indistinguishable. Mickey would kill himself trying to beat a competitor if that's what it took to win. He just happens to be one of those rare people who has too much guts for his own good. Mickey is just unafraid of anything."

My subsequent question caused Fritz to explode into laughter. "Did or does Mickey dramatize circumstances which befall him to his own advantages?" I asked.

"If there was an Oscar for acting in motor racing, Mickey would have won every year that I can remember. Mickey has the uncanny ability to cash in on very bad situations. He had gotten more press coverage about an injury of some sort than most other drivers have received for winning a major race. With those sad blue eyes of his, Mickey has turned all of his failures into success stories.

After setting four world records in 1959, Thompson, center, shares his jubilation with crew chief Fritz Voigt, left, and previous land speed record holder Capt. George Eyston of London.

"My favorite is, one time in the '60s, MT broke his back when he crashed a drag boat—and God knows that the injury was painful. Instead of being concerned about the extent to which his back was injured, Mickey had to make sure all of the wire services got the story first."

With Fritz in a mood of disclosure, I hastened to fire questions that would divest Thompson's protective shield and expose his weaknesses, thus helping to understand why Mickey was the way he was. So far, the time spent with Fritz Voigt was the most rewarding, so I continued: Was Thompson's inexhaustible energy real or was that, too, a form of the dramatic?

Fritz was emphatic in his answer.

"Oh, God no! He would drive himself unbelievably, day and night, on every project we were involved in from the early days of drag racing right up until the time I left, and he still drives himself today. He would drive me, the crews, everyone around his shop. In fact, we rarely had the same complete crews from project to project. Mickey would burn guys out. Even now, he is still burning people the same way. I can't for the life of me figure out how he keeps from driving Trudy, his present wife, insane, the way he operates. His sister, Collene, is the same way. She has been his press agent for years and she has done more good for Mickey than any single person I know. Yet she works the same pattern—day and night.

"It always struck me as peculiar, even during those dry periods we had between building cars or getting ready for some event, Mickey would lay awake nights dreaming up new schemes, new ideas. He could build a whole concept for a race car in his head. I never saw him unwind like a normal man and rebuild energy. I swear to God, he suffered from insomnia.

"Let me give you a prime example. When he sold all of his holdings in M/T Enterprises, a manufacturing company he had built, to Holley Carburetor Company, for close to a million dollars, he could have coasted for many years just sitting on his assets. Not MT, Christ sake no! He couldn't leave well enough alone. It was back to a twenty-four-hour day without even taking a vacation.

"The only really funny aspect to his whole makeup and all of the day and night work was something that his ex-wife Judy told me once. This will prove that even Mickey Thompson is human. She told me that Mickey would drive himself for days and then, playing the martyr, he would leave me and whoever else was working at the shop and force himself to chase after a needed part. But in reality, he would make a quick trip home and scurry into bed, telling Judy not to answer the telephone. Later, he would return without the part."

Fritz cupped his hand over his mouth as a child might when fearful of reprisal for a bit of wrongdoing. A smile broke out on his face at the same time. Fritz was enjoying himself. "I'll bet you a week's pay when Mickey reads this chapter he'll make you pull out half of what I say!"

As we both sat laughing, I began to realize that Fritz's long suppressed and inhibited feelings about the man he had worked for and admired from an ever-present cloud of obscurity were beginning to become apparent.

Fritz Voigt differed noticeably from Mickey in age and in the fact that his emotions surfaced from the depths of repression easily, with little stimulation. He talked freely of his deepest feelings—love, hate, ego, sensitive questions regarding masculinity, and a willingness to make light of his own shortcomings.

"I just raced for the hell of it, for my own enjoyment, never because I wanted or had to prove I was braver than someone else," Fritz commented on several occasions.

It became enjoyable to ask questions of this man and receive truthful answers filled with spontaneity. Mickey's honesty—the one single trait contended to be all-important—was my next question.

"The question of Mickey's honesty must be handled with a delicate and meticulous tone," Fritz cautioned as he began. "Basically, Mickey is a down-to-earth, God-fearing man. However, every man with his type of ego, based on an aggressive nature, is going to have some fragmentations of Jekyll and Hyde within his character."

Fritz seemed as if he was going to engage in a bout of procrastination.

Instinctively I challenged him. "Come on Fritz, tell me straight out, is he honest or not?"

Fritz snapped back with a pointed and defensive answer.

"You have to take time to understand Mickey; that's all I'm saying. Do you want some controversial statement to help make this damn book sell, or—?"

I interjected before Fritz could finish. "I'm only looking for the truth," I stated.

He continued, "There are times, in business, when Mickey can be, and often is, extremely [hard nose]. When he is wheeling and dealing, he projects a will and determination as powerful as when he's driving a race car. Being aggressive causes enemies. Losers in a business deal often aren't granted the luxury of a second chance. Therefore, those who play for large stakes must assume a cloak of hardness. I'm sure that men who have dealt with Mickey Thompson have taken his coldhearted attitudes as being dishonest.

"Another one of Mickey's characteristics that is sometimes misunderstood is his ability to use words, whether it be verbal or written, to his own advantage. Despite the fact that he has garnered only a minimal education, Mickey possesses an almost uncanny ability to twist words to ensure himself a favorable position. Let's face reality, man! When you are dealing for literally millions of dollars on a single

transaction you are fighting for your life, and that's no time to be looking for a person coated with charisma. You have heard that time-honored expression 'nice guys finish last'? Well, in the world of business, as well as the world of motor racing, brother, you better be ready to fight to win or your competitors will run right over your head.

"However, throughout all of this manipulation, in his own mind, Mickey believes what he does and says to be completely honest. His actions are not a willful attempt to commit a fraudulent act. I am convinced that Mickey could take a polygraph test during any transaction he has been engaged in and the needle would never quiver."

Fritz now stepped completely out of character. His voice had a new tone, a note of intrinsic protection for the man we were discussing. Gone suddenly was his vile language and the half-hearted laugh that preceded most of his statements. Fritz was displaying bits and pieces of a long-submerged portion of his nature. He was struggling to relate the truth, but at the same time he was protecting a man for which he had great admiration.

Somewhat later, Fritz sensed his out-of-character demonstration and reverted back by cupping his hand over the microphone and yelling a menial order at his hired man, an order basted with a sauce of profanity.

The truck door slammed, and we continued our journey.

"At times," continued Fritz, "Mickey is his own worst enemy. He will never defend his actions. If the situation is such that Mickey turns hard and unsympathetic, he simply acts without an explanation. Therefore, it's only human nature for those who get hurt to lick their wounds and pour out their frustrations by cursing that bastard Thompson, the prevaricator, the cheat.

"His tendencies to playact, his flamboyancy, and his sometimes exaggeration of fact portrays an uneasy and seemingly surreptitious person. People cannot identify with an outrageous act. Mickey's dramatics—his $300 a throw bets in Las Vegas, renting two 727 jets for his wedding, racing with a broken back." Fritz threw his hands in the air conveying an expression of desperation. "God, the list is endless!

"Normal people can't handle this type of action. Physiologically, a man considers actions of this type a threat to his masculinity and he therefore treats the perpetrator of these acts with distain, calling him dishonest and a liar.

"Those of us who know Mickey consider him as honest as a man with an ego of the size he carries will allow. Most of the guys who claim Mickey has screwed them either have or would work for him again, if the price was right. It's like the fly who escapes from the sticky paper and then goes right back. Mickey's magnetism draws you back; he's a son of a bitch one day, but you'll bust your ass for him the next. Face facts, there are goddamn few virgins left in this world and nobody is perfect."

The tape recorder clicked off with a positive sound. Fritz laid the microphone aside and cocked his body half against the truck's door. One hand rested haphazardly on the steering wheel, the other draped over the seat back. For a long moment he was silent, his mood altered to an unyielding seriousness. His eyes were still warm but reflected a twinge of pain as he spoke.

"Most of what we have said here is nothing more than superfluous crap, isn't it?"

He didn't wait for an answer.

"What has really been your objective since the start is to find out why, after ten years, Mickey and I parted company. And you're interested in having me clear the air about Judy, Mickey's first wife, and his daughter. You want me to do the dirty work because Mickey won't. That's it, isn't it?"

I nodded in submission, adding that the material we had acquired was important in helping me attain my goal: finding the answers to who Mickey was and what made him run. However, I did concede that the question of Mickey's first wife had remained a mystery.

"Our parting began over reasonable enough circumstances. As I mentioned before, I was married to two women, four times. Anyway, my second wife, the one I am presently married to, had moved to Hawaii with my son, in an attempt to get away from the everyday madness of our life. I was commuting back and forth from California to Hawaii about every six weeks. My son was getting old enough to need his father and Mickey and I were between projects. It was during this time that I deemed it appropriate to leave Mickey's employ.

"Before I could make a decision, however, Mickey and I became involved in a dispute over the sale of a small steel-tube manufacturing company Mickey and I owned as partners. I felt it was Mickey's word manipulation playing tricks and, as always, he felt that he was right in his actions. This disagreement sparked some buried feelings I must have been suppressing because I suddenly felt that the insane manner in which we had pushed ourselves over the past ten years was too much for anyone to stand. Also, I had lost a little respect for Mickey and I felt that I couldn't work with all my heart and soul for someone I did not have complete respect for, so I left.

"Several weeks later, I began to see Judy; we had always been close friends and I saw nothing wrong with this course of events. Somehow, Mickey got wind of it and became extremely angry. Again, his ego took over his reasoning powers. The fact that Mickey himself had initiated the divorce action made little difference regarding his thinking. He didn't want Judy as a wife, yet he was jealous of her having a life of her own.

"Many years prior to Mickey and Judy's split, and never dreaming I would be living these events, I argued with Mickey, saying, 'Once a man has lived with a woman, he resents her taking up with another man, even after the divorce is final.' He didn't believe me, but hell, I should know, I was married four times. Now when he was faced with the situation, he knew I had been right."

I questioned Fritz regarding the rumored causes of the divorce. Had he been the leading contributing factor or was a drinking problem on the part of Judy the reason, as whispers suggested?

Fritz's eyes flared as he answered, "I have no intention of dragging Judy Thompson through a mire of crap just because of this book. It's nobody's goddamn business what went on behind bedroom doors. That's the trouble with people nowadays; they're only interested in bizarre details and dirt. Let sleeping dogs lie, that's the way I see it."

Confronted with Fritz Voigt's logic, I let the subject of the discussion drop from sight. He did, however, convey a few more comments.

"I have always felt that Mickey and Judy loved each other at the beginning. They had two children and she was with him on every one of the record attempts. God only knows you have to feel something to put up with that. It's true that in later years Judy developed a drinking problem. It's also true that Mickey is hell to live with at times. There were tears on both sides. But now the wounds are mending. I would never utter anything derogatory against Judy, and I'm certainly not going to comment on my relationship with her; this isn't my or her life story."

Fritz was obviously strained, and judging from his mood I concluded a quick summary would be most appropriate.

"It's rumored that you and Mickey actually fought during your disagreements when Mickey and Judy were first parted," I queried.

"Oh, hell no," was his reply.

"I'm nonviolent, and Mickey, well he's crazy when he gets mad. Hell, when we raced together, I was always pulling him off some guy when his temper let loose. He was like a high school kid.

"The closest we ever came to fighting was one evening Mickey phoned Judy, after their divorce was final, and I answered. Mickey cussed at me for being there, but later he apologized.

"That's all ancient history now. After Mickey began dating other women and finally when he married his present wife Trudy, we buried the hatchet and became friends again. In fact, I really don't believe that we ever really split as lifelong friends. It was just a few years of bickering."

Fritz laughed heartily now.

"Ah hell, we used to listen in when our secretaries would make calls (we were involved in land developing deals during this time of self-induced exile) like a couple of kids. I'm glad I spent those years with Mickey. They were the best years of my life. Ya, I'll tell you, if I died here bullshitting with you in this pickup truck I wouldn't regret my life one damn bit. Mickey Thompson included."

I glanced over my shoulder at Fritz as I pulled out of his garage. He seemed lonely and forlorn. His face was thick, and his torso slumped slightly. He and I both were aware that this might well be the last time the name Fritz Voigt would be mentioned in a story relating to a sport that had now forgotten him. A sport that he could never forget. Ironically, he still stood in the shadows of the man he most admired.

CHAPTER
7

THE DRIVER
AND THE DRIVEN

One year had passed since Mickey and I had agreed on my attempting to find the nucleus of his temperament. It began on a rain-soaked December night, a few days before Christmas. Now, the fresh days of spring, the hot, dry days of summer, and the dullness of autumn had slipped by and rain again pelted the arid California soil.

At this book's inception a timetable for completion was set. One year from its beginning was all the time I had thought would be required to document and compile my material. At the beginning I was filled with fervor and motivated by a passionate drive to become successful overnight. This was a consequential project for an unknown writer. My subject was extremely successful. His reputation was easily expounded, and I found it a simple matter to be tranquilized into a state of self-hypnosis, believing that any promise made would be effortlessly kept.

However, life being an assemblage of compromises, various unforeseen obstacles caused delays and the manuscript and its conclusions remained only semi-completed. For Thompson, whose entire makeup is constituted on a foundation of "completion of an idea on time at all cost," this limbo of an unfulfilled climax brought a bitter taste.

Now, the crevasse of our emotional differences widened. The pressures I had felt, however trivial, during our taping of the Bonneville chapter, returned now in earnest.

Mickey was a man who drove himself and everyone surrounding him unmercifully to reach an objective. Excuses were a sign of weakness. Any attempt to cover up for work that had not been completed as scheduled infuriated him. He once told me, "The one thing that makes me lose respect for a man in an instant is to have him jump in and start working when I happen by, then slow his pace the moment I'm out of sight."

As my work continued, my inner stability began to crumble. At first it was subtle: a few fitful nights, several days away on holiday, nothing of consequence.

Within several weeks, however, the symptoms grew. Instead of spending hours working, my time was spent struggling for ideas. My mind rejected any attempt to cope with the pressures of my task, and images began to flicker across it like a silent movie against an antiquated silver screen. A rapid outpour of meaningless subjects darted across a blank space. Frequently the topics shifted and the difficulty of returning to the original point arose. I developed signs of *folie du doute*, a term used in psychiatry to describe a patient who is assailed by abnormal anxiety when faced with making a decision on even the most elementary, everyday tasks and activities. I could not, or would not, draw conclusions in even the simplest decisions.

Previous page: A peek inside Thompson's Long Beach shop in 1961 revealed Pontiac engines of every type and displacement imaginable. There were V-8s, four-cylinder Tempests, and even two-cylinder engines created by cutting a four-cylinder Tempest engine in half. Some were supercharged while others were not.

Anxiety and apprehension now filled my days. Finally, work on the book halted entirely.

Two months passed from the time I ceased work on the book until a telephone call came from Mickey, as I inevitably knew it would. He questioned me on my progress. His voice was probing, and his words seemed demanding. I immediately became defensive.

Obviously, I was not living up to my commitments in the strictest sense of the word. I had promised completion in one year, yet work had halted at the halfway point.

I became more and more defensive. Sleepless hours resulted in fitful nights. My wife became the bearer of curt remarks, broken dinner engagements, unkind treatment, and many of the things marriage counselors describe as the leading causes of divorce.

Friends called me aside and in cautious, candid conversations told me, "Slow down, you're working too hard." Still pages remained unwritten.

Then one evening, as I sat in my office, the pressures of the task boiling inside my brain, another call came to check my progress. Mickey's voice was again probing, and his words seemed more like accusations than questions.

"When can I read what you have written so far?" he asked. "Soon," was my reply.

"How much more material will you need and how soon will a completion date be in sight?" Two more questions that cut deep. "After all," he continued, "we are now about five to six months overdue on a completion date."

My voice faltered. I remember distinctly that it broke. I had no idea whether Mickey detected it, but it was undeniable, it cracked. At the same moment I began to lie. There was no other way. The pressures of completing the job were astronomical.

"Yes, everything is moving smoothly," I said. All of the material that Mickey was interested in reading was conveniently being edited and retyped. I even went so far as to bring over to Mickey's apartment blank pages stuffed into a binder in order to illustrate how thick the manuscript would be once it was retyped and ready for his inspection.

The respite was short-lived, as expected. The direct pressure from Mickey lessened slightly; however, my own guilt and emotional inability to become motivated increased. Now, what had started as an insignificant flame of depression suddenly became a raging inferno within my mind. Those blockades that hindered thought and idea actually had no place in a book of this nature. Still, day after day the pages remained unwritten.

Summer, with its hot desert winds, came early in June. Cloudless sun-drenched days seemed to stifle my ambition. I could hardly force myself into my office to work. Any reason was sufficient to abandon this now arduous task.

Idle days turned to idle weeks. Mickey ceased calling. I ceased seeing him for any reason other than a few outside business dealings. Despite the absence of each other's company, my feelings failed to change. I still felt his presence every time I attempted to work. My temperament became more intolerant to outside pressures. I stopped seeing friends; I avoided parties and social activities. My sudden fits of temper caused my wife to seek shelter in her own interests. She remained too busy to argue.

By mid-June I felt totally encompassed with the fear of not finishing the book. On advice from my wife I took a week's respite from my work and moved completely away on a holiday.

On my return, the fears, instead of decreasing, increased. All I could muster was an occasional trip to my office, a few random words, and more hours of wasted time.

July arrived, hot and tyrannical. I made, under great duress, a painful decision. I decided to abandon my efforts. My feelings were of utter despair. Even before a final termination was set my spirit ebbed to a state of wretched and forlorn uselessness.

There was no real reason for failure. Portions of the book had indeed progressed smoothly. It was difficult to sit with my own conscience and rationalize my conclusions. I could not pinpoint a single solution, or a justification for my sudden loss of ability. I was convinced, however, that the key lay with the Thompson personality. Some type of barrier had formed, framed by my own inadequacies and anxieties and by Mickey's super ego and forcefulness. When failure was imminent for him, he had fought to overcome all obstructions. I had not.

For several weeks I avoided all contact with Thompson. Fortunately for me he was preoccupied with an off-road race that his organization, SCORE International, was promoting in Baja, Mexico. There were no telephone calls, no meetings, nothing to place me in the position of confessing the fact that I was no longer working on his life story. For the sake of feeding a feeling of paranoia, I continued to rationalize my deception. All the answers seemed coated with candied hypocrisy, adding to a case of hard-core depression. My dialectic thinking was distorted. The one failing Mickey hated most in a man was lying. Yet, for the past two or three months our whole relationship had been filled with falsehoods. It was inevitable that the actual state of affairs would soon be forced into daylight.

The mind has a vastness that can be used as a fail-safe by those who have overcommitted their rationale. A huge storage space has the ability to make vague those things that cause us unpleasant sensations. It is capable of building a wall of amnesia around the problems causing us anxiety.

Consequently, as the days passed and work on the book was allowed to lay dormant, I subjugated myself into a state of moratorium.

Previous pages: On July 9, 1961, at March Air Force Base near Riverside, California, Thompson launched a four-car attack on major national and international acceleration records. Left to right are the two-cylinder *Little Car*, the *Attempt* fully streamlined dragster, the partially streamlined *Assault*, and a '61 Pontiac Catalina. At the end of the day's work, Thompson had broken six national records and eight international records.

Opposite page: Following *Challenger*'s efforts in 1959, and with time on his hands, Thompson went into the speed equipment business. He's shown here machining a crankshaft from a solid billet.

It was late in the evening, on a night in late July, when the annoying peal of the telephone brought reality back into my life. It was unusual for Mickey to call so late; he had always made it a habit never to disturb me after early evening, 7:30 at the latest. His voice was low, and his breath resonated through the earpiece with short, sepulchral bursts of air. As if he had been prompted by a witness, he immediately began to question me about my progress. I had heard him use this tone of voice only one other time since we had begun this project—when he was engaged in the throes of a fierce business deal and about to administer a "coupe de grace."

There was no longer a reason to lie. With heart pounding and a defense mechanism of self-pity leading the way, I spilled forth my story. I could no longer, and for no explicable reason, go on with my work on his life's biography.

I braced myself for the onslaught of Mickey's fearsome temper as a long silence pounded in my ear. Ever so quietly he asked what the problem seemed to be. I explained, as best I could, that it was nothing definitive, a mental block had forced its way into the path leading to the book's completion. And whenever I began to work, fear clamped a lid on my creative process. I explained further that portions of this cessation were caused by fear of failing before a personality who could not comprehend failure.

The long silence was finally broken by a softer, more resonant voice.

"I don't believe," Thompson said, "that you should give up. Not so much for me, but for your own emotional stability. Relenting on a project of this nature could mean the end of your career. I don't swallow that as a convincing piece of logic. But, hey, it's your decision. I trusted you and agreed on payment for a completed job."

In 1962, Thompson's dragster—powered by a Pontiac engine with self-manufactured aluminum Hemi heads—was driven by Jack Chrisman to an 8.76 second, 171.75-miles-per-hour win over Don Garlits in the Top Eliminator final at the NHRA Nationals in Indianapolis. Mickey is seen directly above Chrisman with Fritz Voigt to his left.

50¢

1966
M/T MICKEY THOMPSON

Speed & Custom
EQUIPMENT

Beginning in 1959, M/T Equipment Company became a major player in the speed business. Originally offering pistons and connecting rods, the catalog eventually contained manifolds, blower kits, aluminum hemispherical heads, valve covers, valve train components, and nearly anything necessary for racing. Giant conglomerate Colt Industries bought the company in the late '60s.

His reference was to a large advance he had paid to me at the start of the book project.

"Any money you got from me is yours! I don't want it back. I can afford the price. If there is any change in plans, give me a call."

For a moment after I placed the receiver back into its cradle, I felt lightened. The feeling was only temporary, though, and lasted only through the blinking of an eye. There is no easy way to fail.

An hour passed and still I sat in my office, staring out the window, trying to collect the happenings of the past several months. It had begun as a fantasy and now it had turned into a farce.

One seemingly insignificant—but eventually substantial—development came from the events after my conversation with Thompson informing him of my impasse. It was his show of warmth and understanding. Throughout all the conversations, with rare exception, Mickey's tone had always been firm. All of his business dealings were expressively unyielding. Even in the interviews that I had conducted while gathering information, a mood of eloquence was a scarcity. Only a few times, in his relating of events during his childhood and in his relationship with Dave MacDonald, had Mickey displayed a sensitivity for anyone else's feelings. And for the most part, these experiences had dealt with some form of tragic occurrence. Instead, here Mickey was relenting when he could have stayed true to form and demanded satisfaction.

Only forty-eight hours passed before my pride and ego summoned enough energy to resume work. The pressure eased enough for a second try. I was now in a state of recuperative stability. There was a slight rekindling of the flame that had originally sparked this project. The life of Mickey Thompson was still intriguing and worth recording because he was, I was convinced, a rare breed of man.

The work to be done, which now lay ahead, was to find all of the remaining answers to complete the personality puzzle of this man. No matter what the impediment, he had never submitted to defeat. So, no matter how difficult, I must continue.

As work recommenced, the only stockpile of raw material at my disposal was a solitary tape, recorded at the height of the pressure buildup. It was limited in scope and dealt with an assortment of rather inconsequential questions. However, I hoped it would be a start. I decided to use this tape as a stimulus while Mickey and I discussed events recorded on the tape.

As I threaded the tape through the recorder, there was little indication that this would be the most significant tape of all; that it would create the format for the most interesting aspect of the Thompson story. It would begin the climax I had felt was so distant.

My first question burst out of the speaker like a bolt of electric voltage. I had forgotten what had been recorded. This particular tape had lain dormant for nearly a year. And if I had listened to and discussed the material on this tape with Mickey sooner, then the mental block and the work stoppage may never have occurred. Sometimes writers search for the truth in places where there is no truth, only confusion. Truth is a simple fact and it lies on the surface of our human makeup.

"Why have you always, with very few exceptions, surrounded yourself with employees who have had backgrounds stemming from a subservient existence?" I asked.

Mickey's answer came with a trace of sarcastic overtones. "I am not sure that I like that phrase 'subservient existence.' That means servant, and people who have worked for me weren't servants.

"I have always enjoyed finding people who are down and out, and by giving them a chance, have fulfilled a lifelong goal watching as they overcome their obstacles. For the most part, this type of person appreciates everything you do for them. You take the average guy, who has been fed with a silver spoon all his life or the guy who has never tasted adversity, these are the type of people who won't work as hard as the soul coming up from the bottom.

"You're a classic example of what I was saying," Mickey said as he pointed his familiar, accusing finger at me. "You were never very successful, up to a point, but you had a goal and I thought you could accomplish that goal."

I interrupted Mickey before he could continue, to interject an observation, flipping off the recorder as I spoke.

"Most of your critics, and I tend to agree, say your reasons for hiring underrated help is to bolster your own ego. Is that true?"

Mickey snapped back, "What the hell is the matter with you? Don't you know me better than that!"

He didn't wait for my reply.

Thompson worked with partners to manufacture M/T Rader wheels. The stylish wheels featured an aluminum center riveted to a steel rim and were used on TV's Batmobile.

"Throughout my entire life I have never been, nor will I ever be, a follower. Anyone can trundle along in the footsteps of a predecessor. That isn't for me!

"Whenever I have undertaken a project, I surround myself with people who will accept my ideas and directions without question. The majority of qualified experts within a chosen life, if they're really good, got that way following those who have gone before them. There are very few true pioneers. The first astronauts were by no mean followers.

"Anyway, if you encircle your ideas with followers, then they always have the tendency to do things their way, not yours. And I'm here to tell you that people who work for me do things my way! Most of my accomplishments, the ones that I am most proud of, were built on ideas that were brand new. The type that people laugh at. In fact, there is a certain amount of excitement in being laughed at. It turns me on. I work twice as hard and my blood is filled with a resurgence of energy. I'm going to show those who laughed. And in most cases, I have done what I said I was going to do. You can call it ego, but I call it being different, and for me that's what my life is all about."

The complexion of my author role as a documenter had changed. It was now more aggressive, angrier if you will, than it had been at the beginning. I discovered that in order to extract information from Thompson, it was necessary to force issues. To appropriate his own characteristics proved an effective method of extracting tidbits of comprehension about the Thompson story that would otherwise be reluctant in coming. I became less awed by his manner and more intrigued with uncovering the truth.

"Many of those who have worked for you claim that you are a slave driver; working employees twelve- and fourteen-hour days, seven days a week, was commonplace during projects that you have undertaken," I stated, beginning my new method. "Also, I have heard rumors that you frequently flew into rages when problems arose. Is this a fact?"

Mickey's eyes boiled. He obviously wanted to repel this line of questioning. He appeared irresolute for several seconds before answering. His voice cracked with a hostile tone as he spoke.

"There are no chains around the necks of any of the people who work for me, or whoever have worked for me in the past. They are free to leave any time they want."

"That's a lie," the words blurted out before I had a chance to control them. It was a reflex action. I continued.

"You do have chains around them; most are financially dependent upon you, and most of those who have worked for you struggle against a willpower that is far superior to their own. A will that lesser individuals are powerless to affront."

Amazingly, Thompson held on to many of his projects as seen in this early '80s garage shot. The 1970 monocoque Mustang Funny Car is in the foreground with the *Attempt* streamlined dragster on the shelf above it.

Mickey became furious. It was the first instance in which he displayed the full fervor of his temper. His eyes burned and he pounded his fists as he had whenever he wanted to castigate someone for something he didn't like. For just a split second I pulled back with the expectation of a punch coming across the table that would open a wound on my face as big as the wound I had just opened inside Mickey's ego. The blow didn't come.

"I told you at the very beginning of this book that if a man didn't have the strength of his word, he wasn't worth the powder to blow him to hell. And I would never knowingly lie to you or anyone else. Well, I want you to believe that I'm not lying now, and if you don't truly believe what I'm saying right this very instant, then turn off that tape recorder, keep the advance money, and get the hell out of my life."

He didn't wait for a response but rather continued defending himself.

"Most of the people, guys, that have worked for me have gone on into their own business ventures. And in some cases I have been responsible for the moves. Whenever a man wants to better himself, man, I let him. At the conclusion of every project I have undertaken, guys have learned techniques and ideas from me and then transposed those ideas into stepping-stones toward their own success. Hey, I would never stand in the way of anybody who has the guts to get out and make it. But, let me tell you something, brother. When somebody works for me, they're going to do things my way."

As Mickey continued, his manner changed once again. He slurred his words, a slight California drawl developed, and he used a large interjection of slang. He was extremely sensitive about his lack of education, and most of the time he guarded any of the telltale signs. However, when he became angry, then all pretense was dropped; he became gut level and everyone around could easily understand his meaning. When provoked, Mickey was crude, but effective—very effective.

As our discussion heightened, a reflex action caused me to rewind the tape I had so casually used to begin this present conversation and drop it into a nearby trash can. It had been an insignificant tool at the start, but this unimportant strip of magnetic polyester had unlocked one of the most trenchant aspects of the Thompson makeup. However, the tape had served its usefulness and was now discarded.

Part of the puzzle fell into place. There were those people whom he surrounded himself with. Those people whom we had discussed just a short time ago. There were his personal surroundings of which I now stood in the midst.

His shop, half warehouse, half machine shop, was filled with drill presses, lathes, and the smell of oil; a place filled with thousands of broken and discarded automotive parts. Rooms filled with concluded, then refuted, ideas. Brilliant automotive breakthroughs gathering dust packed into oil-soaked wooden crates. Innovations used as ashtrays.

Adjacent to the shop was Mickey's own personal junkyard. A million-dollar junkyard at that. His most prestigious and expounded project, the *Challenger*, his land-speed-record car, lay in its final sepulcher—an aluminum trailer suffering from terminal oxidation. It was this vehicle that carried Mickey Thompson into the nation's spotlight. Buried, as well it should be, was the burned-out hulk of a race car that once held Dave MacDonald, before, during, and after his crash at Indy. Rust-covered ideas by the hundreds, ideas that had captured no less than 270 world speed records, lay now in various stages of disarray.

Nothing that I observed was uniform. There was no symmetry in his life. His education and his accomplishments were self-kindled. He was alienated, and he hated conformity. The picture of his person began its coagulative process from its beginning as a bowl of mystery.

Continuing, it was clear that Thompson's lack of formal education was, in his own words, a source of mental anguish. It wasn't that he was acrimonious toward higher education, but rather those who used it as a social tool. Once I struck the nerve endings in his ego that invoked the embittered feelings about higher education, Mickey, now unabashed, opened a verbal attack against an obstacle that I feel now was the derivation of his style.

His surroundings, his choice of personnel, and his drive to always be unconventional stemmed from these feelings. Mickey talked for a long time that evening about a subject that had been buried so deep in his subconscious that it had never before seen the light of day.

"Maybe you have hit upon something," he said, a half smile on his face. The same smile that had appeared whenever I stuck at something sensitive, especially remarks and findings conspicuous to his ego.

"Probably this resentment I feel toward, what I consider, overeducated snobs began building in or around 1960. You already know the struggle it was to build my reputation toward breaking the land speed record. Well, afterward, things got much easier and I found myself with more money than I had ever earned in my life. With this newfound wealth I formed Mickey Thompson Enterprises, a speed equipment manufacturing concern.

"By 1966 I was making money hand over fist. On the advice of a few associates I began to surround myself with management personnel—accountants, engineers—I had guys falling over each other, each one overflowing with higher learning. I hired consultant firms. We had surveys, reports, meetings, and every week these managers would emphasize the vast amounts of money I was grossing.

"To this point, before I hired anyone, I had run all of my business ventures alone, aided by a secretary and a lifelong friend who was my bookkeeper. I paid my bills and was fast becoming a millionaire.

"In 1968 I was advised to make several bank loans, bills became delinquent, and old friends asked me why accounts had been left unpaid. Still, my staff assured me that I was making profits.

"One morning, after a sleepless night, the culmination of many sleepless nights, I called my entire staff into my office. They all sat in neatly pressed Brooks Brothers suits, accented with the finest furnishings. Their bellies were full; there was an abundance of pocket money bulging their wallets. Pudgy fingers showed gold-filled fraternity rings and desk calendars were crowded with upcoming social events. For a long moment I just stared at all my work had bought, then I questioned them, one and all. 'You people must think I'm either extremely gullible or just plain damn stupid. Now I want to know exactly why you tell me I'm making money when my creditors tell me I'm losing my ass!'

"Well, there were blank stares, some inaudible mumblings, and an overdose of excuses. We all walked over to the computers. The computers would solve all of the woes? I sat in sort of a half stupor, as I watched buttons pushed and lights flicker. Those little cards, the ones you always see in the insurance commercials, the ones that save money for every policyholder, the ones with holes all over them, well, they flew every which direction. Still I got no answers.

"At lunch I pronounced an ultimatum: either come up with some answers or else some son of a bitch was going to catch hell. Three of my key people never came back from lunch.

"In that same year I discovered a deficit of $1.4 million in my business. Consequently, I was forced to sell Mickey Thompson Enterprises to keep from going bankrupt.

"That's just one example of what I consider overeducated personnel. Since that time, I have hired and fired many guys who do everything by the book. And I ask them why, if they know so cockeyed much about a subject, are they working for me for $25,000 a year? When I dropped out of school to go to work for the *Times* newspaper, several of my close friends were already out working every day. Now, these same uneducated guys are millionaires; some of them are contractors, trash collecting kings, and even junk dealers. That's right, brother, these guys didn't have a lot of fancy book knowledge; they went out and hustled their money.

"Another thing, as long as we are on the subject. For some reason you seem to think that I've never been out of this shop long enough to learn anything but how to eat at a hamburger stand."

This comment was directed at a few remarks that I had made about Mickey's unwillingness to be seen at social occasions.

"I've been there, and I didn't like it one damn bit. When I was married the first time I had the big fancy house in Palos Verdes [a very exclusive area on the Pacific Ocean]. We had fancy parties complete with movie stars, socialites, and Grand Prix drivers. I didn't like it. It didn't help me solve my personal problems. It didn't make my family any closer to me. If anything, it drove us apart.

"The same thing goes for movie stars and those high on the social ladder. For the most part, they bore me. They're a bunch of phonies."

I must have had a rather shocked look on my face as Mickey spoke.

"That's right," he enunciated. "Most of the so-called rich class are a bunch of phonies. The problem with most of those guys is that they think, because of their education or social status, that they are better than anyone else. Well, I'm here to tell you that there is no one person better than another person in this life, especially just because he or she has been lucky enough to make it big."

As Mickey spoke I began to feel admiration for this man. His ways were sometimes crude and inelegant, but I found that they were truthful. His philosophy on life was as simple and as easy to understand as his surroundings: Reach the goals in life that you set for yourself, no matter what the obstacles.

Despite an exterior that seemed rudimentary in nature, there was an interior capable of unscrupulous cunning, limitless energy, and an intrepidness found only in the rarest of men.

Many times I had stood in the cool, dark forlornness of evening, staring at the rusting hulks of racing machines, once fluid motion, now heaped and discarded in what Mickey affectionately called his junkyard. In those forsaken vehicles he had turned the heads of lesser men. He had proved time and time again that a stubborn and ego-oriented mind could battle and conquer minds that had been refined and groomed by the methodization of higher education. He proved that, to the masses of men who admired him, "macho" was the most appealing measure of a man's accomplishments.

Motivated by no other force than his own drive for satisfaction, Mickey had so far mentioned only admiration for his father and a man named Bunkie Knudsen, a one-time czar for Ford Motor Company and an unyielding supporter of Thompson's projects. He was his own man, Mickey stated on several occasions.

"If there was one man that I have fashioned my life after it would be Mr. Knudsen," Mickey had expressed during a taping session.

Still, there was something missing. Certainly, Mickey's racing accomplishments made interesting reading. There had been excitement and drama, and, unfortunately, death had entered the mosaic features of his life. At first glance, there appeared an image of a man who feared nothing, was capable of driving himself and those around him to the point of hysteria, and fit to perfection the role of an American folk hero.

In the beginning of this book I set out to find the source of that intangible spirit that makes a man what he is and not what he appears. My talk had now led me to this point. All of what I had discovered at various stages possessed a feeling of superficiality. The source was buried, yet to be revealed. The question stood: Where to look? The only human emotion that stood untapped was love. Mickey rarely spoke of love, whether lustful, paternal, or the warm and tender love given to a wife or a husband. As I moved on, love would surface, and in it would lie the secret of my quest.

¡VIVA MÉXICO!

In July of 1974 I traveled to Baja, Mexico, with Mickey. This marked the first time I had ever accompanied him without the close proximity of other people. My purpose was twofold. First, and most obvious, I wanted to spend as much uninterrupted time with Thompson as possible because this time period showed the promise of being the turning point of my project. I was now drawing conclusions, beginning to establish personality trends, and could envision a final goal.

The secondary reason for traveling to Baja was to witness Mickey's latest endeavor—a 500-mile off-road race through the wilderness of Baja's famed desert for which he was the major promoter. It was the culmination of nearly a year of labor for Thompson and an organization he had established. Officially, the organization is known as SCORE (Short Course Off-Road Events); however, as is the case with all the endeavors that Mickey Thompson has undertaken in his lifetime, SCORE quickly became known as just "Running for Thompson." Mickey had full control and established such a rapport with the drivers that the organization relinquished its identity to the man who ruled it.

Several enterprising promoters had run similar races within the territorial limits of Baja, Mexico. In fact, at this time, a fierce competition between rival factions had developed to determine who, or what governing body, would control and thereby reap the harvest from events run down the Baja peninsula. Of course, the task for an entirely new organization to emerge victorious was extremely arduous, if not unattainable. It was therefore a direct challenge, readily accepted by Thompson, to prove that it could be done.

Within a matter of weeks, after a firm date for the SCORE race was ascertained from the Mexican government, Thompson's flamboyant methods began to surface. His coalition was to be the most energetic, the most ornate, and the most spectacular. It would be, if Mickey kept control, a new breed of race events to be held in Baja. There were already signs of his intense interest in this event; during conversations we had several days before our departure, a self-induced form of hysteria began to surface. Mickey had scrapped the usual Baja course in favor of a wholly redesigned course. It was to be more rugged, as well as more demanding on both the driver and his machine. As might be expected, however, the prize money would be larger than previous races.

Not limiting changes to merely money and terrain, Thompson interjected computers and space-age scoring devices to aid in keeping tabs on contestants.

Previous page: This is the very professional looking pit area set up on the course by Stroppe's Lincoln team for the car driven by Jack McGrath in the '54 event.

When Thompson entered the 1953 Carrera Panamericana, better known as the Mexican Road Race, he was among some of the world's greatest race car drivers. Bill Stroppe, far right, conducted a meeting of American drivers on his Lincoln factory team. Mickey is at the lower left with two-time Indy 500 winner Bill Vukovich and Jack McGrath directly in front of him. Others include Manuel Ayulo, Chuck Stevenson, Walt Faulkner, Chuck Daigh, and Johnny Mantz.

There would be airplanes acting as spotters, television and national press coverage, and close attention would be paid to those minute details that had been so sorely lacking in events prior to Mickey's takeover. He had coaxed more than three hundred volunteers to aid him in this event: doctors, radio operators, and equipment and men to staff the various pits and checkpoints over the vast wastelands of the course. In every aspect of his first Baja-sponsored race, there would be a certain flair and style that only a promoter of Mickey's caliber could produce. The fascinating point accenting all of the proceedings was the fact that whatever Mickey promised, regardless of how farfetched, he produced.

Two days prior to the first SCORE Baja race found me seated next to Mickey in his plush Lincoln Continental Mark IV. Dawn had not fully awakened as Mickey aimed south through the outskirts of Tijuana, a border town just south of the city of San Diego, California. Our surroundings were gray. A light ground fog rolled and swirled inland after a night's sleep in the sea. Movement took the shape of shadows and everywhere men rose to face another day.

Despite the comforts of our vehicle's all-weather conditioning system, a slight chill seemed to dart through every available aperture. Glancing out of the tinted side window, my eye caught a glimpse of the area's most shameful stigma, an infested pile of neglect known as "Cardboard City." Huddled in mass, among an outcropping of low-lying foothills, were thousands of human beings protected from the elements by little more than discarded packing crates, tar paper remnants, and handmade adobe blocks. Women, children, and grown men suffered the same fate. There were no conveniences, comforts, or shelter to preserve dignity. Pockets of stale air, tainted with the stench of human waste and mixed with the odors of burning wood cooking the morning meal, assaulted our nostrils, even through the protective coating of our insulated embryo. It was difficult to imagine that human beings were actually born into this world of the twentieth century, yet lived and died in a world filled with disease and filth, unable to obtain a better life outside of this environment.

It was a peculiar feeling, too, that here we were surrounded in luxury winging our way to enjoy the pressures of competition when before our eyes people were in a far more real and far more dangerous struggle of life and death.

For the first time in many minutes, Mickey spoke as he detected my stare focused on the passing scene. "We are really lucky that God has elected to bless us with a few favors, aren't we?"

He didn't wait for a reply, which was his usual method when he alone wanted to make a point. "Those people need help, but one person can't do it alone. Every time we come into Mexico, Trudy and I bring food, clothes, and money for those in need, but it's never enough."

I must have expressed a trace of surprise at his statement because Mickey shot back immediately with a candid justification of what he had said. "I never told anyone about my actions here in Mexico before. As I have mentioned on many occasions, I have reached a point in life that allows me the luxury of keeping my actions private. One of the major considerations I took under advisement when formulating the SCORE organization was the amount of benefits the Mexican locals would realize from events conducted in Baja."

These statements made by Mickey, as we drove down the rugged coast of Baja, marked the first time he had unmasked a well-hidden, yet warm and tender expression toward people outside of his inner circle of family and close friends. I had witnessed his expressions of grief over childhood experiences, then his remorse while reliving the death of Dave MacDonald during the Indy 500. But, for the most part, his story had been devoid of any expression of human tenderness. This, I felt, was a significant breakthrough in my quest to find love for this story.

Time passed as we continued toward Ensenada, the starting point of the SCORE race. We waved at the road workers, who were constantly repairing the highway. Most of the highway work in Baja was accomplished by means of manual labor and the workers waved heartily at the gringos as they zipped by in their expensive vehicles, by Mexican standards, on their way to a weekend of relaxation.

We drove through the tollgates, where the language barrier was overcome with the jingle of coins. We passed the fantastic coastline of Baja, with its jagged cliffs that drop thousands of feet to the sea. It was a fascinating place.

The impound area (a place designated to garage racing cars) was a large square in the heart of Ensenada, surrounded by high adobe walls, filled with noise and activity when we arrived. Crews worked on unmuffled engines; gringos huddled in groups, identifying with the participants and gulping Mexican beer. The Mexicans, whose town had been invaded, lined the high walls, enjoying the festive atmosphere.

Mickey had already made his transition from quiet, subdued introvert to his role as leader. He directed, bossed, wheeled, and dealed with the grace of a ballerina, balancing his treatment of individuals as each situation materialized. All of the ruffled edges smoothed themselves after a stout deliverance of Thompson's branding-iron-hot and razor-sharp justice. I was awestruck as I watched the master of personality perform. This was the first time there had been a purpose for my total concentration on observing this man's talent as an actor, father, confessor, con artist, hustler, sympathizer, and, above all, leader.

Tucked away, in a shaded portion of the impound area, rested a vehicle and its driver. They were the most feared competitors of all those assembled. The vehicle was rugged and boxy in appearance, but the workmanship was outstanding. Huge tires implanted a thick, almost out-of-proportion footprint on the asphalt on which it rested. Its roof was actually an aerodynamic wing that caught the wind at high speeds and applied a downforce, supplying traction and maintaining stability. The vehicle stood confident indeed; it had proven itself a winner many times in the past.

The man leaning against the vehicle resembled his counterpart in physical stature and several peculiar idiosyncrasies. He too was short and cubic in shape—his body muscular, his senses keen, and an ever-present half smile denoting a tremendous amount of self-confidence. He was, to quote a phrase, "the bravest of the brave," and had been a winner many times in all types of racing cars. And after all, wasn't winning what everything was about? His name was Parnelli Jones, a name that struck a twinge of fear into the hearts of most drivers who had to face him.

He had competed and won nearly every major auto-racing classic in America. Off-road racing had been no exception. He rode a race car as hard and with as much human tenacity as possible. He was one of the few men Mickey Thompson ever praised for his driving ability. "Parnelli is the greatest competitor I have ever seen, and what makes him so good is his determination," Mickey had remarked to me.

There were times when Parnelli Jones could be arrogant and quick-tempered. His ego was capable of controlling his actions in much the same manner Mickey's influenced his own behavior on occasion. It was only natural that when Mickey began to race off-road their personalities would conflict during the heat of combat. Fueled by press clippings, the two men had developed a so-called feud, which culminated in a near outbreak of violence during a heated exchange when Mickey barred Jones from racing in a SCORE-sponsored event in the United States. Parnelli claimed Mickey had ruled him out because he was afraid to race against him. However, Thompson had refused to race in an event that he himself sponsored, so the matter was dropped.

At this point in time tempers had cooled and a feeling of respect, similar I believe to the gunfighters of the Old West, had matured. Jones was a tremendous draw and Mickey, realizing the power of publicity, was happy that Parnelli was running in this event. In fact, I felt that Thompson admired Jones's ability even more than he was willing to admit.

The following morning, with dew still moist on the ground and the past night's sleep still thick in my mouth, I drove past a wooden ramp from which a freshly painted banner billowed slightly in the morning breeze. It was the starting ramp onto which each race vehicle would mount, then roll down on its long and arduous journey along the back roads of Baja. In the distance, several cars barked a morning reveille, a stray dog howled his retort, and an old bewhiskered, weather-beaten pushcart salesman ready for a busy day glanced a lonely look in my direction as I surveyed the panorama unfolding before my eyes.

I moved some thirty miles down the marked course, past clusters of camper trucks and the scent of coffee brewing on propane stoves. A wave of the hand was the universal means of communication. At an expansive sand wash, where a dry riverbed crossed the road, I stopped, glanced at my watch, and became aware that seconds ago, 30 miles from my location, the first racing machines had begun their duel with the elements.

Surrounded by the rugged beauty of Baja's wilderness, a tin cup of coffee hot in my hands, the deerflies exploring a newfound visitor, I waited for the first sounds of unmuffled exhausts. As a river of excitement flowed through me, the first cars came by my vantage point. Dirt flying, engines bleating an uneven song, drivers and co-drivers—faces covered by helmets, goggles, and multicolored bandanas—gyrated with spasmodic rhythm as they danced over the gnarled road.

Afternoon produced signs of Baja's natural tropical heat and a noticeable thirst etched at my throat. The intervals in which the cars flashed by lengthened. Soon only a few stragglers passed my location. Then there were only the deerflies whining their inquisitive song; the road was silent.

Slowly, methodically, I began to work my way back up the course toward its beginning. The road bore the mark of each car that had challenged its barriers. An uneasy feeling came over me as I drove, keeping a wary eye open for stragglers. Something else gnawed at my awareness. Why hadn't Parnelli Jones passed my position? It was not like this furious competitor to be out of the running so early unless bad luck had caused a mechanical malfunction.

One mile from my original vantage point, I caught a glimpse of a man waving his arms in a desperate motion. As I halted, the man, eyes wide with emotion, thrust his head in the open window. His voice was cracked with tension. Had I seen any emergency vehicles coming up the road? Obviously, he was not conscious of the fact that I had come from the wrong direction; any emergency vehicles would be coming from the starting line in Ensenada.

"No," I shook my head as I spoke. He didn't wait for my obvious question. "Parnelli killed a guy," he said. "Hit him head-on."

Then the man pushed away and joined a group of men standing off to one side of the road. The man who had spoken to me continued to mill about, as if nervous energy and the thought of what had just transpired would not allow him to rest.

Independent from the group, solitary, half hidden by underbrush, squatted a withdrawn figure. Dressed in a motorcycle riding shirt, leather pants, and shin-high boots, the man tossed tiny pebbles into space with an almost mechanical motion. His face was void of emotion, and his eyes shone with an abandonment and desolation expressed only on the faces of the condemned.

As the reality of the tragedy surrounding me took effect, I became more aware of its magnitude.

Crumpled like a discarded container lay remnants of what once was a motorcycle. Lying a few feet away—half covered by a white sheet, bloated by the heat of the day, and still clad in riding gear—was the remnants of a man.

Soon an old Ford sedan rolled to a halt and a man dressed in military attire entered the drama. Behind the officer, an ambulance rolled in, its tires growling on the dirt path. In muffled tones an accounting of events was related. The man who had squatted, quietly tossing pebbles and acting as patron over his fallen friend, moved silently to the police vehicle and disappeared within its confines.

Suddenly the tragic play was over. I stood watching the players leave the stage. Only the deerflies remained.

Later I located Mickey in a restricted portion of the impound area in Ensenada. He stood opposite Parnelli Jones, his head bowed, face set in a grim expression, trying to console him. There was nothing much to be said. Parnelli was visibly shaken. Mickey, more than anyone else, knew what torment followed such an uncontrolled event. It was the second time during our trip into Mexico that Mickey had expressed his inner feelings of compassion. It opened a whole new dimension within his personality. Parnelli remained blameless, but it did not ease the pain. As I observed these two men together, I knew, even without the details of our next tape session, that their lives were now paralleled with the new bond of grief.

Road races in Mexico were not always run on trails. In the early 1950s, a road race was conducted on the mainland portion of Mexico over major highways. Run for nearly 2,000 miles from Tuxtla to Mexico City, it encompassed terrain as varied as any in the world: desert flatlands to high, fog- and snow-covered mountains. It attracted the greatest, most daring drivers in the world, and it took its toll in human life.

Naturally, such a race of insurmountable odds would attract Mickey Thompson. At this time in his life it was the supreme challenge. He had not yet won fame at the Bonneville Salt Flats as the world's fastest man and he had not yet achieved a noticeable amount of financial success. But this was a chance to prove himself, so he went to meet the challenge. The only assets he could offer were courage, determination, and imagination. As Mickey's story unfolded, it was obvious that this would prove to be one of the most incredible segments in a most incredible lifetime.

"My first Panamericana road race was in 1952. Panamericana was the official name given to the event, but the old-timers just called it 'The Mexican Road Race.' I drove a six-cylinder Ford sedan. And by today's standards, it wasn't much of a race car. The only modifications that were allowed consisted of a roll bar and safety equipment. We built giant brake coolers out of sheet metal and we could run [aftermarket] shocks.

"The only possible way I could afford to enter was by getting a sponsor. However, my reputation was what you might call local, and my personal funds were what you might call nonexistent. Finally, I convinced a local Ford dealer to put up one of his most basic and stripped-down sedans, a few extra parts, and some spending money.

"Once we had entered and were on location in Mexico it became starkly obvious just how inadequately the car was equipped. The race itself was a tremendous challenge. The road stretched 2,000 miles through lush green flatlands, over snow-covered peaks, and around thousands of hairpin corners. And there were the long—frighteningly long—straightaways. Miles and miles of two-lane highway where you could go like hell and keep going like hell as long as you had the guts and the car would keep running. From Tuxtla to Mexico City the race was a five-day grind.

"For those who read this book under the age of seventy-six or so, the Panamericana road race may not have much meaning. Most of those who ran in the unlimited stock car class and the unlimited sports car class are either dead or retired. But to those of us who were race car fans back then, the Panamericana is filled with meaning. Drivers with unbelievable style and courage ran this event. Guys like Juan Fangio, Jack McGrath, Bill Vukovich Sr., Walt Faulkner, Ak Miller, Tony Bettenhausen, Ray Crawford, and Piero Taruffi. Man, I get excited just thinking about [those days].

"Well, there were some real hazards, too. The road itself was a killer. In Mexico they use volcanic ash mixed with tar for the road surfaces. When this mixture is hardened by the sun it becomes extremely abrasive and is fully capable of cutting an automobile tire to shreds in a matter of a few miles. The second problem was the local Mexican people. They loved the thrill of a bloody sport and they couldn't help themselves when it came to getting involved. They would line the narrow streets in and around the villages as the cars would pass. So close would they come that they could actually reach out and touch the fleeting machines as they passed, their bodies pressed close enough to feel the heat from the tortured metal."

Mickey was now completely engulfed in his thoughts as he relived this story.

"During the first several years of the race, the winding road had claimed its toll in human lives. Drivers as well as spectators had become victims of the hazards of racing on an open highway. I was young then and danger of such magnitude just didn't faze me. So, we ran the race—recapped tires, short supplies, lack of funds, and sandwiches garnered from other crews and all.

"As we left the starting line in Tuxtla I glanced at my co-driver, Roger Flores, as if to say, 'Here goes nothing.' Roger was just seventeen years old, Mexican-American, anxious, filled with Latin macho, and eager to make a name. Roger would later be my right-hand man building the land speed record car, *Challenger*.

"My stomach was tight and nervous tension dried the inside of my mouth. Soon we were in the mountains and rain began to pelt the windshield.

"From our starting position of twenty-eighth, we had passed all but two cars in our class. The rain grew stronger and a warm soothing sensation crept slowly

The Lincoln team had one hour for servicing at this rented pit stop in Mexico City during the 1954 race. Ray Crawford's winning Lincoln No. 149 is in the center.

over my entire body. A rhythmic pulse beat from my heart to my hands. The rain forced the road to relent some of its harshness and our recapped tires were granted a reprieve from execution. Now, at 100 miles per hour my car seemed to float as if in slow motion. We drifted lazily through corner after corner, wheels cocked in an opposite direction to our drift. It became a ballet, the car responding to each flick of my wrist. The rain remained steady and gradually we caught our competitors.

"I was fascinated by the winding, twisting ribbon of road before my eyes. Most of the nervous tension I had experienced at the start had now disappeared. I began to concentrate totally on my task. Glancing quickly to my right I caught a blurring glimpse of Roger's face. He was smiling.

"We were now 275 miles into the race and behind us lay 1,500 serpentine turns, streaked with black rubber from tires clawing for traction with all the ferocity of a drowning man clinging to a scrap of buoyancy. Just outside of the town of Tehuantepec, we rounded a sweeping turn that exited into the straightaway section leading into the town itself. It was to be our last corner.

"Shortly before our arrival another car had gone off a steep embankment and plunged into a river that ran parallel to the town. Inquisitive spectators began running to see what could be seen. A local policeman, sensing the danger, stationed himself at the exit of the corner to ward off approaching cars. It was a noble idea; however, he had underestimated the speed of a racing car running at top velocity. As we entered the picture, the road was blocked with innocent people running for their lives. There was no place to go! We hit the policeman first and sent him cartwheeling into the air. A freezing cold flashed through my body. I headed for the embankment, not knowing that below another car had already suffered the same fate. The only thought that I could focus on was avoiding the figures darting in my path.

"I yelled to Roger, 'We're going to crash,' I think is what I said or something to that effect. There was no time for Roger; he accepted the chances when he put on the helmet. By this time there was no way to alter the course of what was to happen. We hit some large boulders just before going over the bank. The noise was deafening. The car flipped in the air. Impact tore the transmission and engine completely out of the chassis. Now time and space and events blurred.

"We landed right-side up. My hands had gone through the windshield. Roger sat dumbfounded. A jagged slit in his cheek gushed a mixture of dirt and thick, dark blood. The fear that gripped him excited the flood and it pumped with a quick, pounding rhythm. Roger's teeth were visible through the wound in his cheek.

"My reflexes demanded that I exit the twisted mass of wreckage that only moments ago had been a machine flowing beautifully with a controlled cadence. Fire was my greatest fear. There was nearly half a tank of fuel aboard and that was enough to make one hell of a blaze.

"As I climbed out of the car and fell to the ground, the real terror of this story began. My thumbs, arms, shoulders, and ribs were either broken or cracked in some fashion. In fact, my thumbs were pushed back and rested on my wrists. I crawled up the embankment that we had just crested. A large crowd had now formed and there were military police trying to keep control. The pain was now very intense, and my mind began to fog. In fact, I think you should try a few other sources for information about what happened."

Mickey's statement was not surprising. Part of the pattern that he had established during the writing of this story was to rely on the statements of someone else when he didn't care to discuss a certain subject. When we had talked about his honesty, his business dealings, Fritz, his ex-wife Judy—an unpleasant subject was always counteracted by a defensive statement and the challenge to "ask somebody, anybody, they'll tell you the way it really happened." Now, in Mexico, there was no one to ask. Mickey had been left alone and the only witnesses to his story were the local residents of Tehuantepec, so far removed that now there was not a trace. Mickey's statements, no matter how clouded, would have to be the only testimony given.

For several minutes more Mickey continued evasive conversation.

"*Life* magazine carried a complete spread on the entire accident, it's around here someplace," he said. "They were filming the first wreck, the one that happened just before Roger and I rounded the corner, and could see my crash coming. There was nothing they could do but continue to shoot."

He faltered and his voice dropped as he realized that his final attempt at trying to hide certain events was failing.

"You should check with [author] Griff Borgeson, he had an account of this whole thing in the book about my racing career, he could provide you with details."

I reminded him that Borgeson now lived in Paris and that this was not a book dedicated to his racing career but my search to find the truth about Mickey Thompson the man, and I wanted the details, no matter how garbled, from his own lips. Finally, he relented and continued.

"I lost track of Roger when I finally crawled to the top of the embankment. Several of the military police took me to some type of court. There was, of course, a language barrier; I spoke no Spanish and the court administrators could only speak a few words of English. However, the police officer we had hit as we had started [going] out of control [before crashing] was in the courtroom and was explaining that we had no other choice and that we were attempting to avoid hitting those people who were running across the street when we steered over the embankment. It was at this point that I realized that there had been people below us when we landed at the bottom of that embankment. This didn't have much of an impact on me, though, because the pain had taken over and now all there was in front of my eyes were flashes of yellow pain.

"When the court hearing was completed, I was taken to a small, rundown motel at the edge of town. A doctor was brought in to evaluate my condition. He was a small, dark man with a sweaty face and a bushy, black mustachio. His white shirt carried the traces of several meals and rings of sweat outlined the underarms. He spoke in a strained, broken English, heavy with a Mexican accent. It was useless to try and communicate with him, so there was little to do but allow him to poke and compress my swollen arms and hands.

"After taping my ribs, the doctor, wiping more sweat from his forehead, produced a hypodermic needle and made gestures as if making it clear that his intentions were

to give me a shot for the shock and pain. Withdrawing the needle from a small bottle, the doctor wiped the excess medication from the tip of the needle on his shirtsleeve. A short trail of rust marked the spot where the needle passed. Through my fog I managed to make an emphatic statement that I didn't need any medication.

"Roger appeared, his face covered with makeshift bandages, a pale look in his eyes. He had managed to get a ride back up the course with one of the other crews. He had to hurry, we had no crew members. I was, however, assured that an airplane would land outside of town, pick me up, and fly me to safety. But, for the time being, I would be left alone in the motel room, with the dust, dirty sheets, an occasional rat, the pain, and a strange unmentionable fear.

"Night came with its lonely isolation, but the airplane didn't. I never found out what really happened. Someone said the plane had blown a tire on takeoff and the pilot decided not to make the flight. It could have been that there never was to be a plane and the story was constructed just to make me feel better. My pain had stabilized to the point of a constant, hollow drumming inside my brain."

I interrupted Mickey, who had unconsciously twisted his body slightly to favor the limbs of which he spoke. My question was direct. "What about the people you landed on?" His answer was equally direct, unmuffled by emotion.

"There were five persons killed, so say the reports. I never saw any of them. They were either under the vehicle or they had been cut down by flying debris. At any rate, I saw nothing."

"What were your feelings?" I asked.

"It tore the hell out of me. But you've got to expect and accept accidents when your life is dedicated to driving fast cars. To crash, if you run all-out, is inevitable. My main concern was with my own personal safety. It would soon be dawn and the airplane, my savior, my method of extraction, wasn't coming.

"During one of my lapses of consciousness someone had slipped into the room, probably under the pretext of checking my well-being, and made off with all of my personal possessions, including identification papers, money, watch, all but the clothes I wore."

Mickey accentuated his statements. "Goddammit, I was scared to death. I was alone, the pain attacked my sanity. There were five people dead and who knows what friends and relatives of the dead would feel obligated to do to the perpetrator. I was lying in a filthy bed with five or six broken bones, no money, no phone, no clothes, and a language barrier a mile wide. There was a voice inside me screaming, 'Thompson, get out no matter what!'

"Up until this point, I have always played this chapter in my life low-keyed; in the press and in Griff's book there was only a statement that I had broken some ribs.

Previous pages: Thompson talked his way into a car and sponsorship from Alhambra's Ellico Ford. He had a tough time in the grueling contest, but the Ford survived to serve as a Bonneville push car.

Now, I want to spit out the whole truth. This was one of the most terrifying periods of my life. I feel that I was closer to death in that motel room than in any race car that I have ever driven.

"That night I pulled myself out of bed and began to walk toward Mexico City, 350 miles away.

"The next three days were filled with terror and pain. Voids are the worst thing there is to cope with: periods in time where you cannot remember anything that happens to you. I vaguely recall riding in the rear of a bean truck—crates filled with beans, mingled with the scent of the farm, human waste used as fertilizer, and the cold night air chilling my body. Shock had set in and huge lumps had risen on my hands, wrists, and arms. There was no position in which the pain wasn't intense.

"At one point during the trip I must have been standing by the side of the road. Two men stopped to see if I wanted a ride. Unable to climb into the bed of the produce truck, the two Samaritans, thinking that I was drunk, tried to lift me bodily into the back of their truck. My screams of pain must have unnerved them to the point of stupefied panic. They dropped me in a heap by the side of the road. Despite my cries for help, the taillights from their truck were soon infinite specks bathed in dust.

"During my conscious periods I cursed the Mexicans, the road, my miserable goddamn body for aching so bad I couldn't stand it, my friends for not finding me and taking care of me, the goddamn doctor who tried to stick a rusty needle in my arm, the bastard who stole my money, and finally I cursed whatever form of transportation I happened to be riding on when I realized what was going on. I also prayed a great deal. God, did I pray. I begged God to either kill me or take away the pain.

"During my unconscious periods I sweated, discovered the absolute depths of pain, soiled my pants because there were no toilets, and fell into shock.

"Three days after the accident, two Americans, Bill Toia and Les Viland, found me, foul smelling and in desperate need of help. They drove me to Juarez, Mexico, and from there I was put onto a commercial airliner and flown to Los Angeles for treatment.

"Judy, my ex-wife, met me and saw to transportation to a hospital. News reports had me dead; it was a terrible experience for Judy. She had lived with the fact that I had been killed only to discover that I was on my way home."

Mickey's tone had changed slightly and his words were now matter-of-fact, as compared to the forced tones when he spoke of the crash. He then proceeded with a soliloquy about the following year's Panamericana road race, dropping all interest in the event we had been discussing. It was a trait that I had come to hate. Like an audible press release, it gave fact or near fact, in an irksome series of puffy, guttural utterances void of emotion. Whenever he initiated this method, he had something to hide or had come upon a subject that he did not want discussed any further. I had a sudden urge to turn off the tape recorder and pack up. However, one of the duties of a biographer is to remain neutral and collect the entire story.

"The following year," he continued, "we were back, this time better prepared for what faced us."

Mickey's ego burst forth on center stage and a series of revelations about his personal accomplishments appeared. Obviously, this would be filler material.

"In my second attempt things went better from the very start. Roger Flores was once again my co-pilot and one of his duties, aside from map reading, was to operate a dashboard-mounted movie camera. We were going to film the whole race with hopes of selling the footage.

"I led the first lap, in my class, and we were really running hard through the mountains. In fact, I beat most of the big-bore sports cars (Mercedes, Ferrari, and Lancia). However, we developed an oil leak. Repairs were made, but a 30-cent gasket failed, and the oil leak persisted. We could run hard for only a few miles, then we would lose all of the engine oil. Not having much money, getting oil became a problem. I said we were better prepared than the previous year; I didn't say completely self-sufficient. Anyway, Roger and I devised several ingenious methods of obtaining oil. Simply drive into a local commercial service station, grab a few cans or bottles of oil, fill the car with gas, and before the startled owners could get over the shock of having a real race car drive into their establishment, we would jump into the car and roar away.

"At one point we pulled up to a Mexican local parked on the side of the road watching the race, and while Roger gave him a few words in pidgin Spanish, I drained the oil from his car's crankcase into an old cowboy hat and poured the lubricant into our smoking engine and continued. Not the most subtle way of improving Mexican–American relations.

"We were rewarded for our oil pilfering when I lost control in a mountain corner, after the steering gear broke, and smashed through a stone wall. It looked as if someone put a charge of dynamite under that wall. Man, rocks flew everywhere. I remember yelling at Roger, 'Turn the camera on!' He didn't.

"I never went back to race on mainland Mexico. The Panamericana race was canceled. I'm sure the reason was because too many people died. That was back in '53 or '54, I can't remember which. The next time I raced in Mexico was in Baja in an off-road event in 1969."

In a state of near exhaustion, Mickey rambled for another half hour. Most of his conversation related to anticlimactic sidelights of the two Panamericana races. I began to pack up my tape recorder and call it a night.

As I reached the door to leave, Mickey, now dozing on a huge couch in his living room, stopped me with a sharp retort. "Tom," he said, a deadly seriousness in his tone, "I cared about those people I hit in Mexico. It has haunted me for years. I cried for them, and I never saw their bodies, never knew who they were. It is still a terrible memory. But it wasn't my fault. That's why the Mexican people mean so much to me. I just wanted you to know. I cared, really cared!"

His eyes closed and his hand rested over his forehead; I caught one last glimpse as the door clicked shut behind me.

As the elevator began its descent from Mickey's 17th floor apartment, I stared out over the Long Beach harbor, lights twinkling from the ships moored close to the shoreline. The night felt cold and lonely. I thought of the terror Mickey had gone through, those days after the accident. And how he had tried to hide his feelings up to the very last moment. For him, to show the hurt inside was very difficult. And for some unaccountable reason I thought of those poor unfortunates living in "Cardboard City," just south of Tijuana, those we had seen on our drive into Mexico. Having Mickey reveal the story the way he had helped make my task seem more worthwhile.

THE BUSINESS OF
MICKEY

Autumn came to California, with its foggy mornings, overcast days, and chilly evenings. This was the autumn of the second year of my task, a task of finding the truth about the life of a man filled with contradictions. He no longer seemed to me a mystical knight in shining armor, the world's fastest man. Now he was a middle-aged millionaire who had risen out of the obscurity of a low-income lifestyle to a position of wealth. In this statement lay the contradiction.

My initial concept for this chapter was to engage in a candid exposé of Thompson's vast wealth. Reveal his hidden face—that of a millionaire wheeler-dealer, shrouded in mystery, constantly poised in a game of financial chess, maneuvering for the checkmate thrust.

At first, Mickey cooperated. For hours he hinted about stock options, sponsor money, a dozen corporations he was either involved with as an officer or the controlling shareholder. Admittedly, he was deeply entangled in real estate through a network for worldwide holdings. When I mentioned that rumor had it Mickey had recently executed oil investment proceedings that turned a substantial $400,000 gain for a minimal original outlay, he laughed in the spontaneous, explosive manner that warmed those around him, a laugh that occurred only sporadically during the time that I had been in close contact with him. He even went so far as to plant the seeds of intrigue by admitting that he held, hidden in a location known only to himself, a store of gold.

As I continued to force a probing wedge deeper into the sanctuary of his most closely guarded secrets, my own discontentment began to grow. Feeling everyone would be drawn in by the allure of the subject of money, I became entangled in building an interest in the Thompson dynasty. As quickly as it began, I became entrapped within my own obsession. The Thompson personality, capricious as it is, had no interest in the subject at hand.

Thompson hated being identified with those who established themselves as rich and opulent and clamored for social position. "Money is just something you use as a tool, like a wrench or hammer," Thompson once said.

If he identified with any one image, it was his surroundings. Clad in jeans most of the time, sporting a T-shirt stenciled with some sponsor's product, Thompson produced an enthralling bond with the common man. He truly loved working with his employees, socializing with race car drivers from every rung of the social ladder, or talking with his countless fans at the racetracks at which he appeared.

Previous page: Thompson's mother Geneva was obviously very proud of her son, who rose from a modest upbringing to become legendary in all forms of motor racing and wealthy beyond their wildest dreams.

Opposite page: Thompson's first outing as a promoter was a series of auto shows he dreamed up while in a hospital bed. Beginning in 1960 and running through 1965, the popular shows featured classic cars, hot rods, custom cars, and race cars of all types.

Mickey Thompson presents

THE WORLD OF SPEED!

PROGRAM 50¢

THE '62 NATIONAL AUTO
AND BOAT SPEED SHOW
SHRINE AUDITORIUM
LOS ANGELES • DEC. 7-10

Mickey Thompson
A Champion on Your Side.

Mickey Thompson meets or exceeds every criterion for commercial sponsorship. His accomplishments are real, known and respected throughout the world. His public celebrity is the best; he has earned it. He is articulate and masculine — the intelligent kind of man who engenders trust.

He relates to all age groups. His personal and professional conduct is of the highest order. And, he, perhaps more than most, appreciates the meaning of "performance."

He understands the economics, workings and requirements of business. *(The recent sale of his own $10,000,000 a year business has freed him to give his full time and attention to sponsorship promotions.)* Non-conflicting, multiple sponsorships are sometimes advisable, as all sponsors gain bonus exposure from promotional publicity.

Taken together, these attributes, these criteria will give real punch to the marketing program employing them. Consider your own product-image requirements. Whether your program calls for print, radio, television, direct mail, sales films or any combination of these, Mickey Thompson can be a powerful spokesman.

He will not come to you alone. He brings an enormous built-in audience and an immediately established recognition factor.

Some of America's greatest business firms know the benefits of sponsoring Mickey Thompson. He is at the top of his form and ready to do the job for you.

Mickey Thompson is a proven quality. He talks straight to your customers.

RAPID PACE, INC.
10347 HOYT PARK PLACE
EL MONTE, CALIFORNIA 91733

Across the street from his shop in Long Beach near the docks dotting the harbor, there was a junkyard buried in the heart of the freight warehouse district. Heaped with scrap, the yard is an enlargement of Thompson's own race car junkyard that lay rusting behind his shop. For hours Mickey would involve himself with the three black men who represented both management and the labor force of the yard. They would argue price and talk about building fast cars and how much money Mickey could afford to spend. Everything was relative; the men liked Thompson for who he was, and he enjoyed and respected them.

This same type of friendship existed between Mickey and the countless prizefighters he was continually picking up and helping, down-and-out guys with nothing but their physical attributes to offer. Mickey was an intimate part of their way of life. I discovered that some of his closest friends, families that he met on his honeymoon trip to China, were nearly paupers. Still, these were the people he regarded as special.

It was useless to pursue the intimacies of his wealth. He had no use for discussions about money. When I questioned him about business dealings he would simply answer, "If you are doing a job for a particular sponsor or giant corporation, then those discussions that go toward producing a bond between you and the party you're dealing with are only effective if you keep the party's trust. And you keep their trust by keeping your mouth shut. Even after all of your contracts, good or bad, are completed."

He hated high rollers and big business wheeler-dealers. "I have already told you what I think of most college-educated young executives: They're all followers!"

What about the prestige of being well-heeled? I once asked.

"I've had all that and it's not worth the effort. It's all for show and terribly ostentatious. When I was married the first time, I had a fancy house in Rolling Hills Estates, a very high-rent district on the ocean on the outskirts of Los Angeles. We entertained all the time. I had Grand Prix drivers, governors, senators, you name it. It didn't mean a thing. All that money couldn't buy me happiness. My wife drank; we divorced. My kids had their share of problems. For the most part, money just got in the way."

Mickey did, however, enjoy the money he made in his own eccentric methods. His second marriage, to his present wife Trudy, was one example. He toasted the celebration by renting two 757 jetliners to transport the entire entourage from Los Angeles to Las Vegas. With some rare wit, Thompson is quick to note that there were no high-rolling socialites aboard.

"Who was there?" he shouted. "Most of the people who flew with us were friends I used to throw papers with when I worked on the *Los Angeles Times* newspaper. Friends that I hadn't seen in fifteen years."

Following the sale of his speed equipment empire, Thompson wasn't ready to rest just yet. This flyer explains his value to advertisers, promoters, and manufacturers as a spokesman. Thompson's sister Collene and brother-in-law Gary Campbell handled his public relations.

At times Mickey used his money like the old gold rush kings of years gone by, for completely unpredictable and spontaneous reasons. He would spend to help those in trouble with the same fervor that he would pay an unknown author a staggering sum to record his life story.

Gambling was another enjoyable use for money, and Thompson had an uncanny streak with Lady Luck. For him, winning was effortless. I observed a firsthand account of his abilities on a windy, moonless night in Wendover, Nevada. Wendover is the gateway to the Bonneville Salt Flats and every land-speed-record car has been trailered through this city. However, as famous as it may be as a gateway, Wendover leaves a lot to be desired for nighttime entertainment. One gambling hall is the extent of it.

On the night of this story, Thompson was at the Salt Lake Flats for a twenty-four-hour stock car speed record attempt sponsored by the Ford Motor Company. I was there on assignment for a magazine I was working for at the time. After a day of hard running in blazing heat, Mickey walked through the gambling hall, still clad in his driving suit, on his way to a news conference being held in a small room in the rear of the hall. I walked with him, interviewing him as we walked. As we passed the crap tables, Mickey reached into his driving suit, produced a roll of bills totaling about $1,500, and nonchalantly tossed them onto the table. Judging by the reaction of the pit boss, it was the largest bet the house had had in some time. Without so much as a detached glance, Mickey picked up the dice, tossed a seven, scooped up his winnings, and continued his pace.

In Las Vegas, on his wedding night, Thompson systematically won $25,000. On another occasion, Thompson made a stopover in Vegas, stuffed his total winnings for the evening in his pocket, and then headed for Lake Mead and a record run in an unlimited racing boat. A serious crash sent Mickey to the hospital with a broken back. Unconscious, Mickey missed the woeful expressions of the Catholic nuns who admitted him to the hospital when they found $3,000 wet dollars, wadded in the pockets of his racing uniform.

For the first time in two years I began to enjoy a taping session. Mickey was lying on the floor of his office, his shoes off and four or five racing jackets propping up his head. I sat, cross-legged, next to him, the tape recorder grinding methodically between us. The door opened and John, Mickey's favorite employee, a stocky, dark-haired man with grease and grime from a long day's labor etched on his face, poked his head in to ask a question.

Mickey laughed at the man's facial expression and quipped, "We're not making love in the corner, just taping, and there is more room on the floor."

As the man shut the door, Mickey commented, "That guy will be a millionaire someday because he's got drive and determination. He doesn't know it yet, but someday he'll own more than I do."

Thompson's dominant team of Mustang Funny Cars in 1969 revolutionized drag racing. They were the first to feature narrow frames, dragster-style roll cages, and zoomie headers. In Las Vegas celebrating yet another victory are (from left) car builder and crewman Lil' John Buttera, mechanic John Kranenburg, builder and red car driver Pat Foster, Thompson, blue car driver Danny Ongais, and crew chief Amos Satterlee.

For hours into the night Mickey and I sat on the floor as he joked and mused about his weakness of spending money like a drunken sailor. Most of the stories were showy and carried an air of gaudiness. Perhaps distasteful to some, but it was simply Mickey's way of manifesting his feelings about the overemphasis placed on the value of money. And, as always, when he elaborated on any issue, it was to the point of fanaticism. Just part of his contradictory character.

When racing in Baja, Mickey invariably roared down the Mexican peninsula with $400 or $500, in $50 bills, tacked to the dashboard with clothespins. In the event of a problem, where manpower was a major ingredient, Mickey would wave a fistful of money out the window and help would blossom out of the cactus.

Once, to promote tire sales for a tire company he owns, Mickey wore bow ties made from $100 bills. If a buyer stocked his store with Thompson tires, he would pull off his tie and hand it over to the buyer.

The act of making money was never any real chore for Thompson—to the contrary. Every underestimation or miscalculation, which would have broken a lesser man, inexplicably turned up roses for Mickey. Broke three times and then back to the status of millionaire, Thompson's business ventures held no logical order in their design. He has owned, and still owns, many automotive-oriented businesses, which seems plausible. However, he has also owned hamburger stands, used car lots, ice

cream companies, candy factories, oil wells, cattle ranches, hotels, and giant plots of real estate—all of which he keeps locked in his own secret life, into which he allows no other person.

With the same zeal that he boasts about his extravagances in spending money, he keeps from view the good that he does, which he considers private to himself and those he helps. He rarely speaks of the orphanages he supports, the scholarships paid for every year, friends in debt that he has quietly helped over his lifetime. He has even showed deep personal commitments to drivers who have raced his cars and were injured in the process of competition as well as the families of those who were killed. In a sport where chance is the common denominator and loyalty is infrequent, these acts should be considered noteworthy of a man's integrity.

Still, under hard and relentless cross-examination, Mickey refused to elaborate. In fact, the only path that led to any revelation at all was when we engaged in a rather heated argument and a flare of temper caused some telltale signs to surface. Most of the time he would close the subject with an inconsequential remark about having enough money as not to be forced to give reasons for his actions. Or, if he felt kinder, he would relate another pompous account of how he bought a piece of worthless beachfront in Australia, pumped off the backwater at great expense, and sold out to an unnamed hotel chain at a considerable profit.

It was no use. The dynasty was there all right, hidden by Thompson's refusal to divulge information. For the attentive observer, the signs sometimes surfaced more clearly. The penthouse apartment, the airplane, unmentionable amounts of pocket money, his beautiful wife's Liz Taylor–style love for jewelry. Then, just as quickly as they had appeared, the signs disappeared, like a rock entering a quarry pool, with a dirty T-shirt, store-bought fried chicken, and long nights in a musty garage surrounded by everyday men with sweat on their brows and high-speed machines on their minds. I really couldn't complain about Mickey's reluctance and his evasive maneuvers. It was all part of his total makeup: completely unpredictable.

After an all-night session, I decided over a steaming cup of coffee that sleep and the discontinuing of my meddlesome curiosity into the Thompson method of moneymaking would lighten the burden of my task. I packed up my tape recorder, justifying my conclusion of effort by reasoning that I had uncovered enough information to give the reader a suitable foundation on which to build his own ideas. It made things more interesting. Yet when the gestation period of the gathered information had passed, I began to hunger once again. There were too many questions left unanswered.

Since the beginning of my relationship with Thompson, his opponents had unanimously agreed on two points as a basis for their dislike of Mickey Thompson: he was a blatant opportunist and he used people without regard for feelings. Friends, loved ones, adversaries, whomever he needed—all were included. Well, we're all opportunists in one form or another, so I disregarded point one as inherent to the origin of man and concentrated on point two. Did Mickey use people to get his way?

"You absolutely piss me off." Mickey's statement threw me off guard; it was highly unusual, as he rarely used abusive language. His voice was stern, and his mood was obstinate as he spoke.

"For the past two years," he continued, "you have insinuated that I have used, oppressed, browbeat, and castigated everyone who has ever worked for me or engaged in business dealings with me. What the hell is your reasoning?" He demanded that I name names, places, incidents.

It may have been the haughtiness in his voice or maybe the frustration that comes from trying to pry apart an individual's life for all to see. Whatever the ignition, a fire now burned brightly. I felt hostile and snapped back with my answer.

"Three-quarters of the people I have talked with over the past two years say you use people like race cars, and when they can't do you any more good, you park them. I've even been warned that when this book is completed my turn will come."

Mickey's temper flared up as he spoke. "Let me ask just one question, one simple little question, before you continue. Of all these people you talked to, and obviously you must hold their opinion in high esteem or you wouldn't be saying this, has any one of them told you that they were used up by me, or was their statement based on hearsay?"

Suddenly, Mickey pounded his fist on the table at which we sat. His eyes were fixed directly on mine and for the first time Mickey's temper was aimed at me as an adversary. "Tell me, goddammit!"

I couldn't. There had not been one person who spoke from direct experience; most had related, in half-truths and gossip, their defamation of his character.

"Then," I asked, "how did you gain such a tarnished reputation?"

"Because I have never offered explanations for my actions," he answered. "I think we should differentiate between using someone up as a personal vendetta and being competitive in business dealings. In business I'm ruthless to the point of being unethical. You'll notice I said to the point of being unethical. That's my line, my termination point. I won't lie to close a deal, but when it comes to dealing, I will fight as hard as I know how to win.

"We've talked about this before," Mickey continued. "I do not give reasons for my actions, nor do I make excuses for failures. When I was playing football as a teenager, if I dropped a pass or fumbled the ball, I didn't come back to the bench and complain to the coach that the ball was wet or I was hit too hard. I failed, and if he couldn't comprehend the circumstance, then that was tough shit. Since that time, I have failed for many reasons and on many occasions over the years, but the reasons are my own, as are the failures. There have been times when I have given reasons to protect sponsors. If their products caused me to lose a race or fail to break a record, hell, I'm going to protect them the best that I can. So, I make an excuse. But, for the most part, what I do and why I do it stays right up here." Mickey pointed to his forehead and smiled, his temper now cooled.

"I won't walk across the street to explain my actions even if it means losing the biggest business deal of my life. Also, I won't walk across that same street to change a person's opinion of me. If people don't like me for who I am, then I don't need them any more than they need me. Of course, these are my feelings

about business dealings. When it comes to personal feelings, then I would go to the ends of the earth to avoid hurting someone who was innocent or to undo an unjust wrongdoing.

"All of my life I have felt that if you have a job to do, then that job must be completed at all costs. I have a feeling that this might be a difficult concept for most people to believe, at least in our present age when talking seems to hold a higher level in the scheme of things than action. But, as simple as it seems, this has always been my philosophy.

"There has also been much said about my dealings with the major auto companies, Ford, General Motors, etc. Every car owner, driver, or sponsor wants a piece of the giants. For many years, during the peak racing years and before our

Leave it to Thompson to be creative with his 1971 Pinto Funny Car. The titanium chassis cost twice as much as a conventional one and was powered by a 429 Ford shotgun engine. Driven by Dale Pulde, this car won the AHRA Winter Nationals and was runner up at the IHRA and NHRA winter meets.

present inflationary period and declining car sales, money was no object when it came to the racing teams. It flowed like cheap wine, and ruthless men were ready to stab their best friend in the back to get a share of the action. I was lucky when those big dollars were being spent; a huge portion of them were being spent by Mickey Thompson. Naturally, this set of circumstances caused no end of hard feelings among those who didn't make it. I soon developed the reputation of knocking every company I dealt with and skipping out the back door. Even my friends were taking potshots at me. However, despite the lying and the erroneous statements, my dealings with the giants of the industry were satisfactory for all concerned.

"Sure, I wheeled and dealed and bullshitted at times, but that was the only way to stay ahead. It was a tough business, and anyone who thinks that dealing for unlimited budgets and multimillion-dollar contracts is anything but hard-nosed is terribly naïve. I made it a practice to never discuss my contracts with anyone and if the company I was dealing with did not publicize the fact that I was involved with them, then I never mentioned it to anyone.

"There were times when a sponsor wanted the public to believe that I chose their product because I thought it was the best product for the job and not because I was being paid. This is somewhat of a fairy tale but, unfortunately, money paid the bills, and racing is all bills.

"Rather than defend myself against the absurd number of allegations thrown at me, I just kept my mouth shut and let my accusers draw their own conclusions. When you analyze the people who take potshots at a successful person, most of the time those taking the shots aren't very successful themselves. It's just their own inferiority and inadequate feelings coming to the surface. Being a producer for paying corporations is a competitive way of life, and I'm a very competitive person. If stepping on a few toes to get a job completed was necessary, then by God I stepped. You show me one millionaire, one top executive, who isn't a tough, hard-nosed son of a bitch and I'll show you a guy who was born with a silver spoon in his mouth. I wasn't. I wanted a lot in life, and I got it. Nobody ran up and handed me anything; if I wanted to be successful, then I had to do it on my own."

Mickey waved his hand in my direction. He was getting himself worked up again. The calm that had overtaken him passed and he was again impassioned with releasing feelings that had been pent up for many years. I did not try to restrain him, but rather sat back and braced for the onslaught.

"You're the perfect example of what happens when a person can't cope with pressure and blames everyone but himself," he said. The remark caught me slightly off guard, but that had been the climate of my last few experiences with Mickey.

"When you began this project," Mickey said, "you were filled with great expectations. We made an agreement, a word of honor agreement, if I remember correctly, for you to complete this project in one year's time."

I acknowledged without uttering a sound.

Mickey continued, "I lived up to the agreement by paying you for the project in advance and asked nothing but your word to do the best possible job you could. You gave me that word!

"After several months, you suddenly developed a tremendous guilt complex. I felt this sense of guilt grow and manifest for six or seven months. You weren't doing the job. I knew you weren't. I could tell from the telephone conversations we had, with the stammering and stuttering. What should I have done, cried for you, felt sorry? That's not my nature.

"Finally, you and only you left me no choice but to demand to know what had been accomplished.

"All of the pressure was self-induced, and you were working under a tremendous psychological handicap. It was a simple problem, in my mind, of you not knowing whether you were capable of doing the job that had to be done. I had commissioned you to write this book, giving you a free hand to see, feel, and digest information any way that your conscience felt it should be. You told me that you yourself were convinced that the story would prove that ego was the driving force behind most of man's attainments, mine included. But now you were impotent. You couldn't reach the goal you had set out to achieve. You had no ego to drive!"

As he spoke, I knew what he was saying to be the truth. The most difficult act was to swallow the bitter words without regurgitating. And, as he continued, the clouds surrounding this man's personality, which had hung like a dreary winter's day, began to clear.

"There are times when a man must prove himself as a man. This was one of those times. I wanted you to complete this project for yourself. It wasn't the money. Hell, I've told you before, money doesn't mean a damn thing to me. It was the principle. Abandoning this book would have ruined you as a writer and as a person; losing your self-confidence is a terrible thing. I let you control your own destiny. Never once did I motivate you in any way.

"I cite this as an example because, instead of realizing my motives, you blamed me for all your tensions and trauma and failures. I became the object of your anxieties and inadequacies. When I offered no defense or explanation, you automatically placed me in the position of being a browbeater, a castigator, and a user of people's feelings. That's bullshit! It was you, not me, causing the pressure. In my way of thinking, the difference between you and me is that you gave me your word to produce, and excuses supplanted action and results. I would have moved heaven and earth to complete a project on time because his word is the only truly sacred virtue a man has to offer."

Mickey wasn't quite finished with the shameless expression of his feelings regarding me and this project. I had come to him and offered to document a life that I thought would be of interest to everyone who wondered what made a personality such as Thompson tick. He had agreed to collaborate only at my urging. Now it seemed as if all of the priorities had been distorted. At times I had turned his character into something gross and ugly. Could it have been my own ego and my own fears of incompetency?

Despite his verbal berating, I felt relief because now the pressure was beginning to wane. All of the hidden weight of unfulfillment began to lift. For the most part, he was justified in his denunciation of my actions over the past two years.

It is a difficult matter when your weaknesses are exposed for all to view. You stand naked and without shelter of the all-too-human defense of self-pity and excuse. However, when the truth is expressed in a straightforward, unpretentious fashion, there is little choice but to accept its conclusions.

"If you think you're the first person I believed in," Mickey continued, "you're wrong. I've had a lot of losers, people I trusted and believed could do a job and then failed. And I've had a few winners too. Their successes have stimulated my life. Whether or not this project is a success is entirely up to you. And if it fails, you can offer the excuses for the failure."

With that, Mickey dropped his assault on the problems we had made, and his voice mellowed as he attempted to draw his conclusions into a basic philosophy.

"You know something, Tom, in this country a man has the advantage of becoming anything he wants to, provided he has the drive to do so. Probably, to a great many left-wing liberals and most of the intellectuals, this seems a little on the corny side. But it happens to be true. This is a fantastic place we live in; it was founded on drive and the will to overcome obstacles. I guess that's my philosophy; choose what you really want to do in this life and then fight until your goal is reached."

With a half smile, Mickey's face flushed slightly, and he indicated that we should wind up the session as soon as possible.

He did, however, continue to speak as I packed up. "I'm sorry if I got on the soapbox but, goddammit Tom, people are so damn lucky to live in the United States that they sometimes lose track of reality. My accomplishments haven't been earth-shattering as far as accomplishments go, but I was free to do with my life what I wanted to do. Those goals I did accomplish were what I wanted. Hey, let's break this up before I go out and run for some political office."

It was Mickey's way of joking his way out of a serious subject, when he no longer felt obligated to talk about it.

As the reels of my tape recorder spun with a methodical, toneless whirring, I felt a sudden sadness that this project was nearing its completion. The magnetism of Thompson had drawn me close and its effects were, as I could now see, beneficial. His simple beliefs, which I had scoffed at as a smokescreen behind which he could hide his inner being, stimulated those around him. I had witnessed this firsthand.

His mention of God as the only one he would ever owe an explanation for his actions awakened a sensation in the pit of my stomach that had not stirred in years. At first, talk of God by a man who had gained the reputation of being a self-centered egomaniac seemed frivolous, shallow, and out of place. But, now, it began to carve through the thick layers of skepticism, incredulity, and cynicism. As simple and commonplace as it seemed, here was a millionaire with a basic love and fear of God. Most ego-centered, self-styled millionaires I've known have precious little time for God, except for an occasional curse.

I would miss, also, hearing of his accomplishments. Contrary to his comments about their unimportance, Mickey's enthusiasm and competitive spirit had given the world of motor racing some of its most colorful history.

Thompson wasn't afraid to try anything. Author Tom Madigan, left, was on hand when Thompson introduced his so-called "oxygen" car which used compressed air in place of a supercharger. The setup was installed in Thompson's white '70 Mustang Funny Car and looked promising during dyno testing but basically did nothing on the track.

There was another component, more tangible now than at the start; one that I began to feel may be the key to this entire story. I had felt, for months, that at the completion of the book, my usefulness would terminate and I would be heaped onto the pile of collected and stored history that lay rusting in the race car graveyard adjacent to Thompson's shop—necessary at the time, too valuable to be discarded, but conquered and no longer a challenge. I would lose my identification with the man when his story was completed.

Identification was the common denominator that gave the Thompson personality its individuality and perceptibility. Every man who treasured his manhood, no matter what his position in life, no matter how much or how little monetary value he possessed, could feel a comradeship with the deeds of Mickey's career. After all, he had no special education. He had worked with his hands and fought with only his talents, common sense, guts, determination, ingenuity, and balls. He had made millions, spent and lost millions. Yet he wore jeans and a T-shirt and spoke on a level that every man could understand. There was nothing pretentious about him. Every person who saw him felt a twinge of kinship as he passed. They could yell, "Hi, Mick," and get a nod. He was always family to the underdog!

There was, in these quiet moments of reflection, the ever-present Thompson contradiction. Why wouldn't there be? Each time I had revealed facts that pointed to a trend in his personality, Mickey would reverse position and his character would run toward an opposing path. With the moroseness of concluding this project came the relief of deliverance from a silent pressure that had ghosted my work from its inception—the constant demand of a 100 percent effort every time I sat down to write. Being fascinated by this story was one stimulation; working with the subject was another, more demanding inducement.

One other factor gnawed at my mental computations with the galling pain of realism. It was a factor that demanded to be satisfied. Was the picture, which presently lay developing in the fluids of evolution, a true portrait? Certainly Mickey had, by this point, placed a blanket of influence over my judgment. His case was strong; he believed in who he was. The problem I would contemplate in the final weeks of my close association with him would be to remove any reasonable doubt from my conclusions. I had to rationalize all of the information as presented and disavow his influence. I must believe, without reserve, that this story and the statements of my subject provided a clear and true picture to the reader. All would be lost if any shadows of disillusionment or untruthfulness appeared.

My final statements must not only be a manifestation of this man's achievements but also perpetuate their legitimacy.

ALWAYS INNOVATING

It was Christmas Eve and winter had come to California. Though inclement, the weather was mild by national standards. My task neared completion, but an ominous cloud of doubt still hung in the skies of my mind. It became a concentrated effort to press on. Always there was the temptation to deliberate the evidence.

All those defamatory comments spoken by Mickey's enemies, which I had blatantly disregarded when uttered, now haunted my conclusions about the Thompson personality. A biographer must choose his source of truth and ultimately stick to that choice despite all hinderances. Mickey had been my source since the beginning. Now there was a flicker of doubt that threatened to kindle the flames of uncertainty.

Throughout the long night of Christmas Eve and far into Christmas morning, while traditional dreams of sugarplums danced in the minds of sleeping children everywhere, and adults gathered their thoughts into a peaceful state, I sat, my eyes transfixed on the black mesh of a tape recorder speaker as reel after reel of two years of labor doled out a review of a man reliving his life. Outside my office window a fierce wind blew ominously as an omen of the discord in my mind. The wind of contrariety scattered my thoughts like so many leaves.

By morning, as exhaustion forced a respite and sleep could no longer be denied, final conclusions now seemed more distant than ever. There was even a scent of unconcern wafting about as my old friend procrastination came to share the hours.

Several days later I took an early morning breakfast with a group of Thompson's associates in his newly founded off-road racing association (SCORE) to discuss their emotional responses to their business relationship with Thompson.

The meeting was held in a small café located in a cove, near the coast town of Malibu, where a well-mannered Pacific washed within a few yards of the restaurant's broad panoramic windows. The aroma of hot steaming coffee and frying bacon filled the room. It was warm and friendly, and the ocean, tended by a band of velvet white seagulls, lapped the shore, content within itself. Over eggs Benedict, sweet cinnamon toast, goblets of mimosas, and coffee, we talked.

Spokesman for the group was a man named Sal Fish, the man Thompson had personally appointed to take over as president of the SCORE organization. Of Italian extract, Fish was young, dynamic, intelligent, and an impeccable dresser with finely polished manners. What a contrast to Mickey's coarse, rough personal technique.

It struck me in a peculiar way, as we sat talking, that over the past two years, Thompson and I had never really socialized in an intimate atmosphere. We had

Previous page: Mickey and Danny Thompson raced Big Red at Baja in 1972. The Chevy C20 was two-wheel drive, big-block powered, and as fast and tough as you would expect a Thompson rig to be.

Opposite page: Despite being well into his fifties, Thompson was always ready for another challenge and another race.

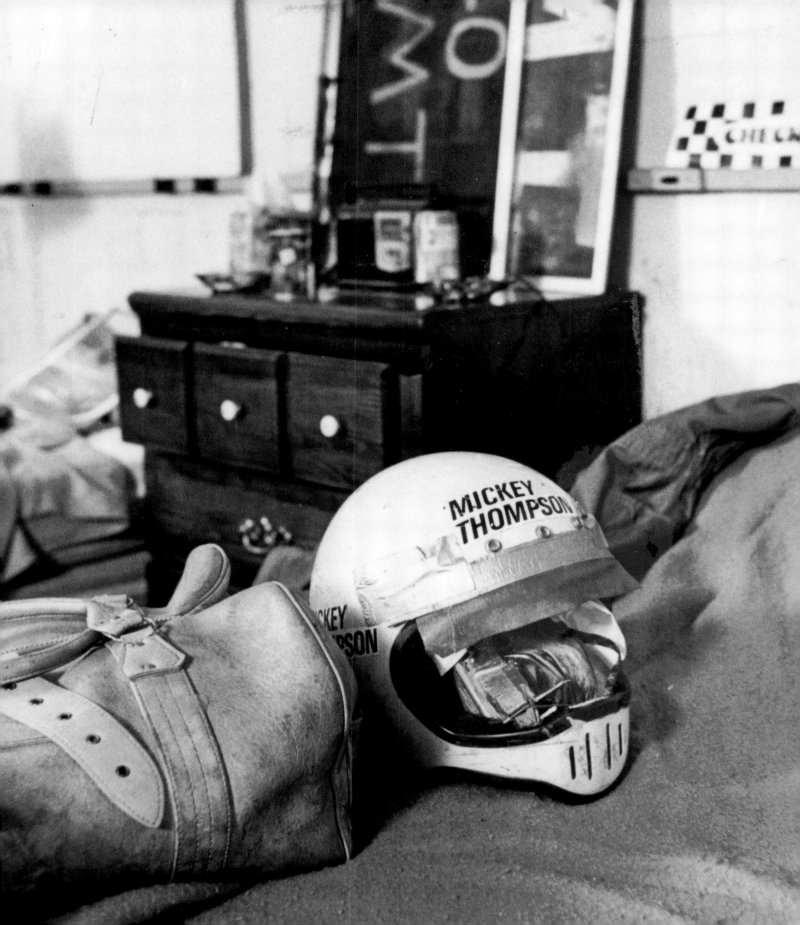

only eaten dinner together once in a restaurant, a rod and gun club located on the flatlands outside the city of Long Beach. The area was surrounded by oil fields and the feeling of country sportsman was tainted with a perceptible air of artificiality. The only forest was one of oil derricks and storage tanks.

While waiting for dinner, instead of quiet conversation, Mickey challenged me to a shooting duel with 12-gauge shotguns and clay pigeons. Aside from this one occurrence, whenever Mickey took nourishment in my presence it was either out of paper cartons or cooked by his wife, Trudy, at his apartment. We always worked while eating. Mickey's pattern of etiquette was coarse; he often talked with a mouthful of food. He would often eat nauseating combinations: huge bowls of ice cream and peanut butter and chocolate sundaes before dinner was served, and he spread mustard over everything he ate—chicken, steak, roast beef, cookies, everything.

As our meeting developed in intensity, it became obvious that Mr. Fish had been subjected to the same self-induced pressure that I had felt. His pressure was more pronounced in many ways because of the short period of time he had been associated with Mickey and their close proximity to one another during times of stress.

We discussed Mickey's methods of commanding leadership and how he had overcome tremendous physical and mental obstacles in building the SCORE organization from obscurity to the leading force for the promotion of off-road racing events, both in the United States and in Baja, Mexico. This, of course, was only one feat in a lifetime of such tasks. There was no question that Thompson had spent his adult life turning dreams from ambiguous and enigmatic visions into successful, paying realities.

Fascination, of a sort, ebbed into the conversation as I was astonished by the similarity of conclusions drawn between Mr. Fish's feelings about his relationship with Mickey and my own judgments. As we spoke, there developed a marked admiration shown by this young executive for his employer. He also brought forth one refractive

When Thompson went off-road racing, he realized that the best part of the show was being seen only by rattlesnakes and tortoises. He decided to promote closed course versions of off-road racing and founded Short Course Off-Road Events (SCORE).

glint from the prism of Thompson's personality that had, up until now, remained transparent. Mr. Fish confessed that during negotiations with giant industries and their representatives, political figures and corporate attorneys, Thompson was brilliant, no matter how difficult the proceedings.

He never procrastinated or stammered under pressure. And what was most important, Mickey fought for the views he thought were most important, never relenting, unwilling to deviate from his belief in what he thought to be fair. I remembered, then, that this was a man with a doubtful education, a man on the streets who was at home in a garage, working on an invention of speed. Again and again I was reminded of Mickey's remarks one night during a particularly difficult taping session.

"Tom," he said, "we are all so goddamn lucky to live in America. If a person has the incentive and will power, they can be anything they set their mind to."

After the breakfast, which lasted nearly four hours, I left the restaurant alone and walked the beach for several miles. I wanted to be alone so that I could sort out, fairly and justly, all of the facts that swirled like demons in my mind.

It's not without reason that I had cultivated a warm, although, I felt, one-sided, respect for Mickey and his accomplishments. On the other hand, I had the responsibility to the reader to reserve final judgment until all of the facts had been digested in my mind.

The sun broke through the clouds as I walked, and the surf, sand, and sun seemed to tranquilize my turmoil. As relaxation uncluttered my thoughts, my imagination presented the question: If the time and year were different, what would Mickey Thompson have done with his boundless energy? Surely, he would have notched a larger place in history. In years past, those who possessed a limited amount of education but an abundance of courage and initiative were presented with more opportunities. Many years ago, when the individualist was more respected, Thompson would have been settling the vast land that is now the west, and the west may have been the ideal location for a man of his character. He excels in those attributes necessary to survive as a plainsman, gunfighter, land baron, or gold financier. However, his was a time when the world turned to a society based on groupism, with the individualist becoming a dying breed.

With the sun shining in my eyes, I suddenly got a lump in my throat. Under my breath I cursed Mickey's antagonists. I also cursed my own weakness for allowing petty human frailties and bouts of insipidness to cloud my judgment and hamper my task. A warm feeling of respect and friendship for Mickey slowly surfaced as I walked the beach, with the sun, surf, and seagulls lending a natural harmony to my state of mind.

More than twenty years before NASCAR promoters started talking about installing "soft walls," Thompson invented and patented the Hydro-Barricade. His water-filled injection-molded barriers were developed for use on racetracks and highways.

The feeling had been lying dormant, I'm sure, for many months, and now it had been awakened. Experience with the Thompson personality had taught me caution, however, and not to expect reciprocated feelings. The friendship I felt would remain one-sided. That didn't matter. I was not, in the short period of my involvement, a significant milestone in the overall picture of Mickey's life, and room for personal warmth in his life was limited. My feelings were significant because I solved the deep-rooted problem of establishing a basis of truth. I believed wholeheartedly that the accumulated facts within these pages were accurate and truthful to a point of satisfying my own conscience. The search was over!

There is not one of us who will not be ripped apart when battered by a constant attack directed at the soft underbelly of our personal weaknesses. During the past two years, I had joined with Thompson's antagonists in an attempt to capitalize on his human frailties. As the reader will testify, this has been a brutal assault.

Without losing his composure, Thompson accepted this onslaught while painfully admitting his faults. He conceded that he was a vicious business dealer. I had exposed the fact that he tended to act, better than a Hollywood star, to gain sympathetic views. Through bitter tears, Mickey talked openly about a tragic marriage and about a daughter who had cast her father from her life. He spoke, with unabashed sorrow, as he relived the most terrible trauma any man can live, the horrendous experience of being the instrument that takes the life from another human being.

Throughout the entire ordeal, Thompson rarely offered any defense for his actions, and he had given forth information that he was not compelled to give, but rather produced voluntarily in order to add credibility to this story. I discovered that shortcomings and imperfections, once exposed, were not the true image of this story. It was Mickey's accomplishments that made the story believable.

"It could only happen in America." Words to preface an old, forgotten late-night movie. Words too corny for our present day and age. This might be the billboard of Mickey's life.

"Mickey Thompson, a ragged paperboy from the streets of Los Angeles (enter a tattered little boy, the image of Mickey Rooney, dressed in shorts, sweatshirt, and baseball cap, shoes without laces and a sad but determined look) would someday rise to become the world's fastest man." It had an exciting ring to it!

Maybe it was true, as one of his close friends had said, that Mickey had been born in the wrong time and that our modern, sophisticated way of life had passed him by. In many ways, he really did belong on the late show, cast as a hero, to serve as a break from reality. Regardless, he accomplished what he had set out to do in his life, no matter how vain the motives were thought by some, and he never backed away from a fight, nor had he deliberately taken unfair advantage of a competitor. He had remained an individualist and asked no man for help. And all that he possessed, he truly earned. That's all that is really important in any story: a man's integrity. At least, I believed so as I stood alone contemplating my conclusions about one man's life. I didn't give a damn about those who would scoff at my findings. It was a rewarding experience to be a part of this story's unfolding.

The occasion was a gala banquet in honor of SCORE's first year as a full-fledged sponsor of off-road racing. It was a particularly rewarding evening for Mickey, for it had been a tremendous struggle, as he overcame a recession, sagging sponsorship money, inflation, gasoline shortages, and critics to make his new organization a success.

This would mark the last time I would observe Mickey Thompson before the completion of this story. It would be my last time to see him in his natural habitat. The evening was so typical of his story.

Hotels that cater to banquets of this type are notorious for their plastic, superficial, pretentious atmosphere. However, this night, in this particular hotel, there was an exception—Mickey was alive and in complete control. He seemed to be dwelling within his absolute domain. Thompson had built his organization from nothing and this banquet was the culmination of his energies. He moved now at a fever pitch, as had been his pattern at the climax of every project since the beginning.

Dressed in a very expensive suit, he bulled his way through the throngs with a flair and flamboyance reminiscent of a diplomat rather than the underdog fighter, a role that he sometimes portrayed. With acute precision he greeted each and every individual who had gathered: drivers, sponsors, wives, members of the press, officials from Baja, Mexico (who had flown in specifically to establish a rapport with Thompson to ensure his continued support in sponsoring races in Mexico), and the unknowns. How he enjoyed talking to enthusiasts who have never received recognition. A simple "Hi, how ya doin" and Mickey would win a supporter for life.

Only once during the evening did I speak to Mickey, and then for only an instant. His face was slightly flushed, and he was genuinely excited. For those of us who knew Mickey it was enjoyable to observe his actions. As he gripped my hand he quipped, "Tom, I want this to be the best banquet ever held." And before the evening drew to a close, Mickey's hope became reality as the SCORE banquet attained a position very high on the list of "good times had by all."

Thompson's radical rear-engined, 160-miles-per-hour off-road Chevy pickup was the cover subject of the June 1975 issue of *Off-Road* magazine. Author Tom Madigan served as editor of *Off-Road* for more than nine years.

With wine flowing and laughter filling the room, a rather touching scene developed. Several members of Mickey's staff and many of the drivers who raced in his off-road events presented Mickey with two awards. The first was built from a pile of bits and pieces of broken and destroyed race cars, most of which were fragments from mishaps that occurred during races sponsored by Mickey's organization. Welded together, the conglomeration resembled a modern sculpture created in a junkyard: pieces of fenders, engine parts, broken wheels, gears, and a host of amalgamated scrap. Everyone concerned laughed until their tears splashed like the wine they drank. Then, the same friends presented Thompson with a plaque that bore the inscription "To Mickey Thompson, Champion among Men." It was their way of expressing thanks for his effort in making SCORE a success. Touched, Mickey stammered an almost inaudible response.

I felt a personal surge of kinship for those who had given Mickey this recognition for his endeavors. I knew firsthand that the struggle had been a difficult one. Despite the fact that he claimed he was undeserving of any type of reward, I knew that below the surface of his conscious mind his powerful ego ever-yearned for satisfaction.

A period of thirty days passed from that night until these final pages were completed.

There was much time spent in the usual methodical logistics of completing a manuscript—editing and rewriting. Of course, Mickey expressed disapproval of portions of the story that he felt were either a distortion of facts or proved to be immaterial to the reader. He objected to several statements made about his mother, his first marriage, and comments made by Fritz Voigt. As had been his policy all of his life, when Thompson wanted changes, there was no use in arguing. The only recourse I have to the readers of this story is to say that the changes made in no way affect the meaningful content of this story.

There was, at this time, a moment to pause and reflect on the events that had transpired over the past months of struggle to reach this point. And for the biographer, at least this biographer, reflection provided a cooling of tensions.

It would alter the trajectory of this book if the plot suddenly became dramatic. Most of the drama occurred during circumstances more significant than the one that follows. Only one singularly serious consequence remained, that being Thompson's reaction when the completed manuscript would be dropped into his hands. It had been agreed that I would reserve the right to hold back the last few pages so this reaction could be recorded without any interference from Thompson.

However, this time had not arrived as yet. And there were still a few quiet days remaining for some judicious pondering.

For myself, reliving the life of Marion Lee Thompson had brought forth one irrefutable fact. In a country where men are allowed the freedom to live and fulfill all the goals their imagination and ingenuity can create, there are few barriers that are impregnable. All that is required is courage. For this fact I am most proud of Mickey Thompson. In most cases, his goals were fulfilled using only courage, and whether his goals were significant or trivial in the eyes of the reader, the point is that they were important to him. And by exerting a supreme effort to reach each level of his life, these pages of testimony are due.

As if I attempted to prolong the inevitable, I drove the long way to Thompson's shop the day delivery of the manuscript was due. Bypassing the major freeways, I wandered down streets that exposed the heart of the Long Beach inner city. There were hundreds of small business buildings, most of which dealt with the automobile—parts houses, auto dealers, garages, welding shops, and gas stations. All seemed relevant to this story. Mickey, as a young race car builder, and later the world's fastest man on four wheels, had frequented many of these establishments in his constant pack-rat–like quest for bits and pieces to build his dreams.

There were also examples of shattered dreams as I drove on. Bars, smelling of stale beer, crowded every available space. In them sat incomplete men, who drank to prevent reality and their human failures from forcing a foothold in their tired minds. Ladies of the street strolled the avenue, their body movements offering a subtle invitation to a form of escape for those who could not find love.

The sight of disadvantaged children playing in front of equally shabby tenements made me want to stop and shout, "There is still a chance to save yourself, all you need is courage!" Life here was a struggle, filled with frustration. Frustration expressed by a multitude of statements in graffiti, scrawled with jets of spray paint on every available wall. Further down the road, two black men stood handcuffed in the center of a group of policemen. I wondered how they had tried to release their frustrations.

All of these sights and sounds suddenly became very important because these were the people I wanted to reach with this story. Mickey had stated many times during our conversations that he wanted to help young people overcome situations of poor environment and make something of their lives.

"If just one kid," Mickey said, "reads this story and realizes that he can better himself by determination and guts, then I'll be happy."

In the beginning I had viewed my task of recording Thompson's life as a simple yet painful one because of the continuous stream of contradictions involved in his makeup. Now I saw that task completed. It had, in many ways, been painful. But it too had provided me with one of the most rewarding experiences of my life. Thompson was truly a remarkable man. And what was even more astounding was the fact that despite our intimate relationship over a period of two years, he had maintained his stature of aloofness. He had remained a stranger!

Author Tom Madigan, left, and Thompson saw a lot of each other when Thompson was deeply involved in off-road racing and beginning his stadium racing series. Their relationship dates back to the days when both were involved with Lions Drag Strip.

I sat for a prolonged period of time in front of the sky blue, unmarked warehouse that served as Thompson's business offices and racing headquarters; my heart was filled with honest apprehension. My palms were wet with perspiration. Truly, I did not relish the conclusion about to be drawn. Knowing all too well Mickey's ability as a compulsive nitpicker, I had no real idea what his reaction to this story would be.

As I entered, Mickey was seated at his desk, a telephone in one hand and a french-fried shrimp dipped in mustard in the other. He motioned me to sit down by waving his head and the shrimp simultaneously. I laid the leather-covered holder containing the manuscript on his desk. He smiled as he hung up the phone. We exchanged cordialities and he looked sternly at the packet of bound pages. He did not open it to examine its contents.

From his desk drawer he withdrew a check for payment of the project, handed it to me, and shook my hand. He then expressed a few words to the effect that he was glad the project was completed and said he would be in touch with me in a few days regarding any changes that he might request. There was no fanfare, no ceremony. A simple transaction; his life recorded on pages of paper for a check. The project was over. The anticlimax of the proceedings hit me like a solid blow.

Changing his tone, Mickey expressed excitement over his latest project, an all-new revolutionary off-road race car that he was in the process of building. He previewed the vehicle's concept, complete with renderings in full color.

Stuffing the check in my shirt pocket, I fabricated an excuse, a pressing business commitment, and turned away, moving toward the door. As I reached the door, Mickey's voice sounded soft yet with more authority than I had ever heard before.

"Tom," he said. "Thank you for what you have done from the bottom of my heart." His eyes were cast onto the drawings lying on his desk.

All I could do was nod my head in recognition. A great weight, the weight of disappointment, lifted from my body. I knew nothing else would ever be said.

A cool breeze dried the perspiration my nervous tension had created. I stood, staring through the chain-link fence that surrounded Mickey's million-dollar junkyard. For the second time I reviewed the relics of his greatest triumphs that now lay rusting. Every experience was there. The *Challenger*, the burned-out hulk Dave MacDonald had driven, all of the dragsters and Indy cars. Some good, some great, and some failures. Nonetheless, they all had their moment of glory. And, although rusting and unused, they were not actually discarded, nor forgotten. They were in limbo. It was with these disconsolate hulks I now identified. I too had experienced my moment of glory and now I fell into the classification of completed projects, to be stored but not forgotten.

CHALLENGER II REDUX

BY TRAVIS THOMPSON

Not all of Mickey's relics, it turns out, were doomed to remain forever in the limbo of his junkyard. Some of them—the truly precious ones—were plucked out, sweated over, stripped of their rust, and released back into the world for another shot at glory. You've just had the pleasure of reading one such resurrected artifact. Another recently blazed its way across the sparkling white surface of the Bonneville Salt Flats, to the end of the course and triumphantly back again; a beautiful blue blur that finally, officially, claimed for the Thompson family the elusive piston record that Mickey had pursued so doggedly.

When the late Tom Madigan decided to revive this book in 2018, he planned to conclude it with a brief glimpse at the remarkable story of the *Challenger II*, one of the many junkyard vehicles he'd walked by after delivering his final manuscript in the mid-1970s. Dismissing this vehicle in their interviews as a "car that never came close to breaking the record," Mickey told Tom that he'd given up on the project after breaking his back in a boating accident. But, predictably, he hadn't really given up on anything. Not having the piston record left too large a scar on his psyche. The man who held more automotive records than anyone else alive or dead didn't have the one that mattered the most to him, the one that had put him on the map. That uncomfortable truth was left sitting there, like a pebble in his boot, for almost thirty years. In 1988, the constant irritation prompted him to do something wildly uncharacteristic. He called up his son Danny and asked him if he'd be interested in partnering with him on a full restoration of the *Challenger II*.

For Danny, the call was a revelation. His father, whose worst moments had all involved watching his friends die—sometimes horrifically—on the racetrack, had spent years actively discouraging his son's career in motorsports. In the early days, he'd used his industry connections to sabotage Danny's attempts to gain sponsorship.

Later he'd settled into a pattern of simply refusing to help him in any way. If there was to be a Thompson racing dynasty, he decided, it would be a reluctant one; two generations of men forced to tough it out on their own.

And Danny, to his father's consternation, was fine with that. He didn't have his old man's knack for self-promotion, but he was just as fast behind the wheel. While Mickey was known to go wild on the track, Danny was more restrained, precise, and consistent. He started out in motocross, where parts could be had relatively cheaply, and systematically advanced through to Super Vee, Formula Atlantic, and Sprint cars. On the few occasions when Mickey and Danny raced against each other, Danny won more often than he lost. The *Challenger II* phone call seemed to him an acknowledgment of that, a long-delayed acceptance of his talent and accomplishments. Mickey still wanted the piston record, wanted it badly, and he now believed that his son was a man fit to help him claim it.

Above: Danny Thompson and his crew arrive on the salt for the first day of Bonneville's annual Speed Week in August of 2018.

Previous page: An overhead shot of the *Challenger II*'s aerodynamic profile. The names of the 2018 crew, as well as their counterparts from 1968, are hand lettered onto the transmission access panels.

Above: The *Challenger II* in impound before its record-setting return run. Crew members are given just four hours to prepare the car.

But that didn't happen. The infamous part of the Mickey Thompson story, the aspect mercifully left unexplored in this book, is his 1988 murder. The *Challenger II* had already been given to Danny by then. It was housed in pieces in the back racks of his shop in Wilmington, California, with initial plans for a grand restoration sketched out across dozens of late-night phone calls and torn-off scraps of notebook paper. After the Speed King's funeral, his son locked the car away, exiling it once again to automotive limbo. Tragedy had torn this family of racers apart before, and now it had struck again, this time with a terrible finality.

And yet. . . a pebble in the boot can be an awfully irritating thing, especially if it happens to be hereditary. Danny spent almost twenty years walking by the trailer that contained the remains of the *Challenger II*. It moved when he did. From the shores of Long Beach to the mountains of Colorado, it was there in the background, quietly chaffing him. He knew that the vehicle—originally designed by Kar Kraft, the skunkworks division of Ford responsible for the GT40—had been a technological tour de force when it was first drawn up in the 1960s. The

Above: A photo of the time slip generated during the *Challenger II*'s final run. The 2¼-mile speed was a full 20 miles per hour faster than any of the car's previous attempts.

Above right: The *CII* with its bodywork off following the 406.7-miles-per-hour AA/FS record run in 2016. The streamliner made it over the line, but the overall speed was badly hurt when a needle jet was lost in the barrel valve.

Opposite page: Mission accomplished. Danny Thompson gestures towards the press after his successful record-setting run

construction itself also was immaculate. A who's-who of Southern California's most legendary hot rod fabricators including Pat Foster, Tom Jobe, Bob Skinner, and Nye Frank all had a hand in its creation. But that was four decades ago. The modern outlook was grim.

The *Challenger II* in its current state was, in a practical sense, useless. Both engine bays were empty. What was left of the steering system, stopping system, and fueling system universally violated modern safety standards. Many other essential components were missing, having been gradually sacrificed at the altar of race-day necessity sometime over the last four decades. Most concerning of all was a profound lack of space. The car, by design impossibly narrow and sleek, had no room to swallow the necessary modifications and upgrades. It would be far easier, Danny thought, to simply build a new car from scratch.

But a new vehicle, however fast, would never be the *Challenger II*, the car that his father had entrusted to him. The frame was still good, as was the streamliner's beautifully hand-formed aluminum skin. There was potential there if he was willing to grind at it. By now he'd spent a lifetime in racing, working on dozens of cars from Baja trucks to Indy racers. He thought he probably could do it in a year if he could find the right help and get the necessary funds together. Perhaps two if he ran into major problems.

Eight years later, a full five decades after the *Challenger II*'s original construction, Danny lowered himself into the car's cockpit for one final run. It was impossibly cramped inside, every spare centimeter had been sacrificed to upgrades and mandated safety modifications. His whole body shook, vibrating to the tempo of the two massive Hemi V-8 dry-block engines that sat in front of and behind him.

On the starter's signal, the car leapt away from the line at an unprecedented speed. He passed the 2-¼-mile flag at 372 miles per hour, nearly 20 miles per hour faster than he, or anyone else not powered by a rocket, had ever gone before. He surpassed Mickey's 406.6-miles-per-hour mark with more than a mile of salt to spare. When he reached a rate of 428 miles per hour, a gust of wind blew the back of the car off course, and he spent the next thousand feet skidding sideways, wrestling with the steering wheel to prevent the streamliner from spinning out of control. He got the racer straightened out again somewhere past the 4-mile mark, and resumed accelerating, trying to make up for lost time. The warning lights on his instrument panel screamed at him, but he ignored them. The car would never run again. This last pass was the only thing that mattered.

When he finally pulled the chutes, Danny had no idea what his terminal speed was. He'd been too busy to glance down at his GPS. He steered the *Challenger II* off the course, scrubbing momentum with the car's handbrake. Once he'd slowed down to 90 miles per hour, he popped the canopy, desperate for fresh air untainted by nitro. Its job complete, the *Challenger II* gradually cruised to a stop. And its driver waited. Recovery crews typically arrive within thirty seconds, but that's an awfully long delay when there's fifty years of history resting on your shoulders. As his team members ran towards him, he shouted one question: "How fast?"

Fast enough. The overall piston-powered land speed record now stood at 448.757 miles per hour, and for the first time since 1960, it belonged to a Thompson.

ABOUT THE AUTHOR

Ironically, a man whose family never owned a car made a career of writing about auto racing. Like many of his generation, Tom Madigan was introduced to the world of racing by Indianapolis 500 radio broadcasts. His family moved from Ohio to Southern California in the early '50s where the racing and hot rod culture convinced Tom he'd landed in Paradise. By the early '60s he was even racing his own fuel dragster.

The thing Tom liked most about racing was the stories. He loved narratives and history, and he was anxious to share them. In 1967, a chance encounter with a customer of the nursery where he worked led to a job offer at Argus Publishers. At Argus he would write about cars, wear clean clothes, and not have to dig holes for tree planting. Soon Tom became Editor of *Motorcade*, earned a staff assignment at *Popular Hot Rodding*, and eventually edited *Off Road* magazine for nine years. In 1972 he published his first book, *The Loner* about Tony Nancy, a man he knew well from racing his own dragster. His outgoing personality made it easy for him to become friends with his heroes including Dan Gurney, Parnelli Jones, James Garner, and Steve McQueen. He went on to pen award-winning titles such as *Edelbrock Made in the USA*, *Fuel and Guts*, *The Chrisman Legacy*, and *Follmer: American Wheel Man*.

Nearly ten years ago, Tom was diagnosed with cancer. I've never seen anyone fight so hard or so long to beat this dreaded disease. His bravery took him through radiation, surgery, and chemotherapy. His perseverance saw him write three more books while undergoing treatment; he dedicated his Follmer book to his doctors. We talked frequently by phone, and no matter how much he was suffering, we'd always have at least one big laugh during our conversations. Darlene, his wife of forty-nine years, stayed by his side through thick and thin. The disease isn't pretty and some of the treatment even less so, but Darlene's love and support never wavered. He passed away in March 2019 at age eighty. His final wish was that this book be published.

— Greg Sharp

ACKNOWLEDGMENTS

The following credits go to those fantastic photographers who stood out in all types of conditions to capture the action. This project could not have been attempted without them: Greg Sharp, Steve Reyes, Don Gillespie, Danny Thompson, Collene Campbell, Bob McClure, Don Nickles, and Lou Hart.

It takes tremendous effort and dedication to complete a project like the Mickey Thompson story, and in this case I had more than I could have ever imagined. I would like to offer a special thank-you to the following people who helped make this effort possible: Collene Campbell, Zack Miller, Greg Sharp, Danny Thompson, Dave Titchenal, and Lydia Ulrey. Finally, to my loving wife Darlene, who has been my rock. Not only did these people help with the labor of the project but they also supported me in my ongoing battle with stage-four cancer. I will never be able to repay their efforts.

INDEX